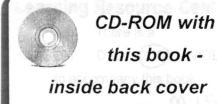

CD-ROM with

this book -

inside back cover

Recording Credits

Adam St. James: guitar, vocals and narration, drums and
drum loops, bass, Hammond organ, engineer, producer
Patrick Doody: drums and percussion, engineer
John Falstrom: bass
David Mathis: keyboards
Debbie Seitz: background vocals

ISBN 0-634-06562-9

HAL•LEONARD®
CORPORATION

7777 W. BLUEMOUND RD. P.O. BOX 13819 MILWAUKEE, WI 53213

018 971

Visit Hal Leonard Online at
www.halleonard.com

TABLE OF CONTENTS

1 *MIDI AUTOMATED MIXDOWNS*

Musical Instrument Digital Interface, or MIDI, is only a couple of decades old (created in 1983), but its inception revolutionized the way music is played and recorded. While it's easy to get lost in the endless possibilities MIDI that offers (the extent of which is too deep a subject to cover in this book), everyone can benefit from understanding its basics and incorporating some of its simplest applications. In addition, it's one of the most adaptable equipment options around, as the even the earliest MIDI instruments can still be used alongside modern MIDI devices, even though more advanced functions have been added to the MIDI language since those early days.

MIDI is most often used with electronic keyboard instruments, but it can also be applied to or controlled by drum machines, guitars and other melodic instruments (with the proper interface), sequencers and—in what is perhaps the most useful application to the recording engineer (and if you're reading this book, that's you, bro)—signal and effects processors and mixers. MIDI data contains information and instructions that MIDI-enabled devices can understand and follow. The most basic of these instructions are "on" and "off" (or "note-on" and "note-off," in MIDI-speak), "pitch" (or "note number"), "start time," and "duration." There are many other parameters that can be controlled via MIDI as well: pitch bends, controller data (such as vibrato, volume, panning, etc.), and instrument or effect selection and changes, to mention just a few.

Even if you're not planning to have or use keyboards in your studio, it's worth your time, effort, and investment to learn the basics of MIDI and set yourself up with some MIDI devices (particularly a sequencer and possibly a controller), because MIDI can do incredible things for your mixes. If you're using a computer—or hard disk-based recorder—you can set up a MIDI sequencer to automate your mixer functions, including volume, panning, and more. You can also use MIDI to control your effects for on-the-fly changes during mixdown.

Sequencers come in both hardware and software versions. If you're already doing computer-based recording, learning your recording software's built-in sequencer functionality (your recording program probably includes a MIDI sequencer) should be no problem. And if you're doing most of your work on a stand-alone hard disk recorder, you can still install MIDI sequencer software in your computer (whether Mac or PC; programs are available for either) and have your computer automate the mixes that, until now, you've done manually. Some of the best-known MIDI sequencing software programs (or programs with sequencer functionality) include Cakewalk, Steinberg's Cubase VST, Emagic's Logic Audio, and Opcode's Vision.

Anyone who has ever experienced the task of automated mixing will never want to go back to the Stone Age (or is that the Stones' Age?), and be forced to mix by hand. With a MIDI sequencer, a good manual, and a few practice runs, you can make the machines do all those previously impossible-without-six-hands changes to your mixes, while you simply play producer (yep, that's you, too, bro), and enjoy the professional-sounding recordings you could never before attain.

TRIANGULATE YOUR MONITORS

The proper placement of your monitor speakers is essential for creating your best mixes; but so many home recording buffs give this less than a moment's thought, and end up just shoving the speakers wherever they find room. But that's not you, right?

Desk-sized monitors—those that most home studios have—should be placed approximately three to four feet apart (or even more for larger speakers). They should also be about three to four feet from your preferred listening position, so that you and your speakers are positioned to form an equilateral triangle. In addition, your speakers should be as far from each other as they are from your ears, which will allow the sound from each speaker to reach your ears simultaneously. Failing to have adequate speaker separation during mixing may rob you of the ability to discern optimal pan-placement of your recorded instruments, causing your mixes to end up sounding dense and one-dimensional. Even sitting just a couple inches closer to one speaker than the other will degrade your ability to pan instruments accurately. Understand? Wait, there's more…

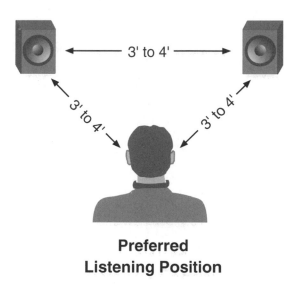

**Preferred
Listening Position**

Bass response will also be enhanced the closer a monitor speaker is placed to a wall. In addition, a monitor speaker placed close to a wall or on the floor will have louder bass than a monitor speaker placed on a speaker stand (a phenomenon called "diffraction spreading," which can add as much as 4–6 dB bass boost). This of course means that when you listen back to your mix on another system, you may find your mix *lacking* bass, because, during mixdown, the bass response of your monitor system fooled you into either turning the bass frequencies down or leaving them flat. But when listening on other systems, you will notice that you actually needed more bass in your mix to achieve your desired results. In other words, if your speakers are too close to the wall, your mix in the studio might sound totally ballsy; but everywhere else it might sound comparatively castrated.

Also, you may find that the optimal placement for monitor speakers is when the tops of the woofers are level with your ears in a normal listening position. Mixes played through monitor speakers placed lower than this level will seem to have lost some bass, which may fool you into unnecessarily turning the bass up. Conversely, speakers placed higher than a normal listening position will cause your mix to sound erroneously bass-heavy, which might cause you to needlessly turn the bass down.

Other things to remember: do not to restrict the airflow of your monitor speakers, and do not place them in a position that would cause their output to be reflected by glass, mirrors, metal, or any other hard, reflective surface. Basically, use common sense about the placement of your speakers and you'll be fine.

3 CD-R? CD-RW? HD? DAT?

Now, how you gonna save those finished mixes? How are you going to distribute your music? You've got an abundance of choices these days, and they've all got their pros and cons. Inexpensive CD burners are fast taking over where expensive DAT recorders used to rule in many studios. But, cheap as they are, who wants a thousand CD-Rs—which are writeable only once—which include only one or two demo mixes each lying around? Who wants rewritable CD-RWs since they cannot be played on standard CD players (although they can be read by DVD players)? Who wants the MiniDiscs, which almost caught on with the masses, but in the end, didn't.

Another storage option would be the removable hard drives, but these won't help you distribute your music. You could even go with a Jaz or Zip drive—if you still have one of these essentially now-obsolete devices sitting around—but again, how are you going to share those files with your band members? There's always DAT, but those units are totally outmoded when compared to today's plentiful and inexpensive CD burners. Besides, DAT tapes aren't as cheap as blank CDs, either.

Really, some type of CD burning capability makes the most sense today. Your computer may already have a burner installed—if so, you're set. If not, I'd skip the DAT, removable hard drives, etc., and go straight for a reasonably priced burner that will handle both CD-R and CD-RW functions (while you're at it, you might as well get something with DVD capabilities, which is fast becoming essential in today's world). Of course, you'll have to check your computer or stand-alone recording deck's specs to determine exactly which burner is right for you, as well as any additional accessories you might need (SCSI cable? SCSI terminator?). Note: it's crucial that you have the capability to burn your CDs at 44.1 kHz, or the standard CD players won't be able to play them; so make certain that your system will support this spec.

A couple of years ago, your decision regarding which storage option to purchase probably could have been based on your budget, but not so now. The prices of all of the above-mentioned goodies are now meeting somewhere in the middle—or even somewhere south of the middle. There are lots of name brands to choose from; but since I am very happy with the external burner that I recently purchased, which was put together by a small shop that specializes in burners for recording studios (and which I bought for less than $150, including shipping, over the Internet), I highly recommend checking out burner options other than those offered by the big names.

Obviously, with all the brands of recorders, burners, and recording software out there, each application will be specific. Due to the limited space of this book, I can't advise each reader on which devices are right for their situations. So do some comparison shopping—online, through catalogs, in person at wholesale and retail outlets—and ask lots of questions; particularly if you need help in understanding the technology involved.

4 SHACKIN' UP

Need some type of connector? Go to Radio Shack. Yeah, cheesy as the place sometimes seems, they got their start selling serious electronic components, cables, and connectors. Chances are they have what you need, and it will probably be cheaper there than at the nearest "Best City Circuit Buyer," or whatever the trendy audio-video-supply-superstore near you is called these days. Hey, even pro engineers buy stuff at Radio Shack from time to time.

5 BACK DAT UP, DUDE

Back up to DAT (despite my previous dis on DAT in tip #3)! Just make sure your DAT machine and your recorder are both set to the same sampling rates. If your DAT recorder only records at 48k, make absolutely sure you've got your hard disk recorder or computer-based recording system also set to 48k when you track. If it's not, you'll face incompatibility issues between devices and lose data in the transfer, which will lead, at the very least, to less-than-satisfying DAT masters—if not completely useless, unplayable files. Besides, again, CD players can only play files burned at 44.1 kHz.

6 WHY DAT'S NOT COPYING

When attempting to copy from DAT to DAT, such as when you're trying to back up your DAT masters or make digital copies for everyone in your band, you might find making more than one copy problematic. That's because, in order to combat music piracy, consumer-level DAT machines are manufactured with a feature that prohibits multiple copying. Known as the Serial Copy Management System (SCMS), these machines will allow only one copy of your DAT tape to be made; and in some cases, no copies are allowed (in which case you'll get a "prohibited" message, particularly if using an older DAT recorder or a DAT master that was made on an older DAT machine).

If you run into this roadblock, but really need to make copies of your DAT master, you'll need to buy, rent, or borrow a pro-level DAT machine, as these machines are made without the SCMS feature. You'll recognize a pro-level DAT machine by its multiple sampling rates, and it may also have both S/PDIF and AES/EBU digital interfaces (while consumer-level machines usually have only S/PDIF). In fact, if the DAT deck accepts an XLR cable, you can be pretty sure it's a pro-level machine, as XLR is required by the pro-level recording standard AES/EBU.

7 SEQUENCERS AND EFFECTS

Getting your MIDI sequencer to talk to your signal and effects processors can be a frustrating procedure; but the end results are worth all the pounding your patience might take. Similar to the concept discussed in tip #1, this tip is concerned with automating your effects for easier, more professional mixes—specifically, getting your MIDI sequencer to talk to your effects units in order to achieve this.

I know, I know—you haven't looked at the owner's manuals to your expensive delay unit or compressor since you bought them. But it's time to stop wasting those sophisticated tools on mere basics. Remember, the art of recording is an ongoing learning process, and here's your chance to exponentially improve your recording skills—and your recordings themselves—in one easy (yeah, right) step.

If the effects device has MIDI In and Out/Thru jacks, get out that manual and look up any info on MIDI controllers or connections—or any mention of MIDI whatsoever. Chances are good that your unit will accept and follow MIDI controller data—most modern units do. That means you can have your MIDI sequencer turn the reverb up on the lead vocal during the chorus, then down again during the verse, while simultaneously adding some slap back to the snare drum, a bit of chorus to the background vocals, and a bit of doubling to the guitar—all while you concentrate on whether or not your CD-RW is burning this great mix.

MIDI-compatible effects units usually allow assignment of a MIDI controller (or several) to an effects parameter or patch. Look in your device's owner's manual to determine how to assign a MIDI controller to the desired effect parameter (such as the reverb level, chorus depth, amount of delay, etc.). Once you've made these assignments, you can use your sequencer to record the changes you want to make during your mix: just run through those changes manually while the sequencer makes note of your actions. Then, after you've learned how to transmit the controller data back to your effects device from your sequencer or master keyboard (and of course, learn to sync your recorder), you can let the sequencer handle your effects units automatically. It's not easy, and it won't be without some serious irritation, but again, the net result is a greatly improved final recording. And that's what it's all about, right?

8 SMPTE TIME CODE

In order to sync two recording decks, a sequencer, a keyboard, or almost any other kind of device, some sort of time code is essential. There are several time codes in use today.

The standard time code that has been used for years throughout most of the recording industry—as well as among musical equipment manufacturers—is SMPTE (short for Society of Motion Picture and Television Engineers). There are actually several types of SMPTE time code, due to the differences in American and European video, film, and television standards, as well as the issue of color or black-and-white. If you're working on music-only projects (i.e., not syncing your music to visual imagery), you should use the *de facto* SMPTE time code: "30 non-drop" or "30nd," which was traditionally known as "30 fps (frames-per-second)." Because some devices feature different choices, check your owner's manuals, then set all devices to the same SMPTE frame rate.

Because SMPTE is an audio signal, it can be recorded, re-recorded, distorted, etc., just like any audio signal. Many devices can serve as SMPTE time code generators. To use SMPTE, you'll need to dedicate a track to it; but presumably, you'll essentially be gaining "tracks" by using MIDI or by syncing recording decks—that's why you're messing with time code in the first place, right?

Today, SMPTE is largely an analog thing; so if you're using analog tape, "stripe" it (lay down time code from beginning to end of the entire tape without interrupting the process) before you record anything on it. Rely on your most accurate time code generator as your master; all other devices will follow this time code as "slaves." Use either track 1 or 8 (for an eight-track recorder), or 1 or 16 (for a 16-track recorder), etc., so that your time code bleeds over onto as few adjacent tracks as possible. If possible, the track next to the time code track should be left blank.

Be sure not to distort your SMPTE time code, and do not use EQ on that track. Print the time code fairly hot (–6 to –3 dB), so that the signal can be heard by all devices that rely on it. Don't use noise reduction on the track; make sure to turn off DBX noise reduction (which usually defaults to always on). Allow some start time or "pre-roll" on the tape before beginning your first song—at least 10 or 15 seconds, if not more—as the various devices that will be syncing with the time code need a few seconds to read the code and "lock up." Also, you may want to avoid beginning the time code at 00 hours, 00 minutes, 00 seconds, 00 frames (00:00:00:00) and start instead at, say, 01:00:00:00, because some machines may have trouble reading all zeroes.

Of course, MIDI devices operate on their own time code: MTC (MIDI time code) or MMC (MIDI machine code). Fortunately, most MIDI devices today can automatically translate an audio SMPTE signal to MTC. Of course, if you're working primarily with MIDI, you may be able to use only MTC for your entire project and not worry about using SMPTE at all. And if you're working entirely in the digital audio world, your devices probably use a time code called "word clock"—a more accurate measurement of time than either MTC or SMPTE, and often required by digital audio devices. If so, life just got easier. Lucky you.

RECORDING SOFTWARE, PART 1:
AUDIO & MIDI SEQUENCERS/RECORDERS

Digital recording has revolutionized the music industry, allowing home studio enthusiasts to afford and use equipment—largely in its software reincarnation—that would have cost tens, if not hundreds, of thousands of dollars twenty years ago. Most top pro studios have gone to digital these days too; the endless possibilities of digital recording made that inevitable. Sure, there are those who still insist that analog (tape) recording sounds better—and there are plenty of studios and products out there for those diehards. But there is simply no denying that digital recording offers more for less, and with an almost indiscernible difference in sound quality. Steve Vai—like many other top artists—has stated that, while he does prefer the sound of analog equipment, there is simply no matching the ease of working in the digital realm. I've watched Vai at work in his home studio where he's got a digital Pro Tools setup.

If you have yet to set up a digital studio, there are many options available to you in terms of the basic recording software packages, sometimes referred to as digital audio or audio/MIDI sequencers, from which you can choose. First, understand that there are three types of digital studios: computer-based studios (known as digital audio workstations, or DAWs), digital stand-alone recorders (those recording decks without built-in effects and other goodies), and digital studios-in-a-box (those recorders with built-in effects and other goodies).

Note that for the best possible recording and playback performance on a DAW, you'll want either two separate hard drives or you'll want to partition your hard drive so that the recording studio software has one drive to itself, and the actual audio data resides on another separate hard drive or partition.

For this tip, I'll focus on DAWs, as well as a few of the most popular recording software programs DAW users have to choose from. Your best options include:

- **Pro Tools by Digidesign** (http://www.digidesign.com). The most widely used recording software in professional studios, Pro Tools comes in numerous versions, beginning with an entry level package Digidesign currently offers everything from a free download off their website to full-blown professional systems which cost in excess of $13,000 (very sophisticated potential), and available in both Mac and PC versions. There are probably more compatible plug-ins (see tip #11) for Pro Tools than any other DAW system.

- **Sonar, Cakewalk Home Studio, Cakewalk Guitar Tracks, Cakewalk Express (and others) by Cakewalk** (http://www.cakewalk.com). Cakewalk products are extremely popular in both the home and pro studio worlds. Cakewalk makes a variety of recording studio software packages for DAW users geared toward different needs, such as their Guitar Tracks packages, which were created to ease the shift into computer-based recording for notoriously anti-high-tech guitar players (and others more comfortable with acoustic instruments than with high-tech keyboards and computer programs). Available in PC versions only.

- **Logic Platinum, Logic Gold, and Logic Audio by Emagic** (http://www.emagic.de/home/news/index.php?lang=EN) The three Logic packages, designed for various levels of sophistication and price, are also popular with many artists and studio owners — both pro and home-based. Logic products are largely customizable by the user, a popular feature among such devotees as Peter Gabriel and John McLaughlin (who uses Logic live on stage instead of a guitar effects rack). Emagic products came in both Mac and PC versions until the company was purchased by Apple in 2002; so all future versions will be Mac only.

- **Digital Performer by Mark of the Unicorn** (http://www.motu.com). Digital Performer is a powerful Mac-only recording package that does not place limitations on how many tracks you can record, as do most other recording programs. With Digital Performer, your track count is limited only by your hardware. And guess what? MOTU sells the hardware to expand your system, too.

- **Acid Pro by Sonic Foundry (now a division of Sony Pictures Digital)** (http://mediasoftware.sonypictures.com/). Acid Pro (which I also discuss in the tip #10 on looping software) is actually a powerful Windows-based recording program with no limits on the number of tracks. Like most recording programs, Acid handles both audio and MIDI. Acid is another very popular choice of recording software; and because of its strong looping abilities, it's very popular in the dance music world.

- **Cubase and Nuendo by Steinberg** (http://www.steinberg.net/en/index.php). Cubase has gone through several evolutions since first introduced. The latest edition features unlimited undo/redo and other functions that make all audio editing essentially non-destructive, meaning you can *always* get back to the version you had before you tried to get tricky and then messed it all up. As in many of the above-mentioned programs, many of the functions of Cubase can be automated, which is a great plus at mixdown. Nuendo, marketed not only as an audio product but as a cure-all for all multimedia applications—including broadcast, film, video, and more—is a more sophisticated (and expensive) package that rivals the highest-end Pro Tools systems. Available in both Mac and PC versions.

- **Cool Edit/Adobe Audition by Adobe Systems** (http://www.adobe.com/products/audition/main.html). Cool Edit, a popular digital audio editing platform from a company called Syntrillium Software, was morphed into Adobe Audition after Adobe Systems bought Syntrillium in 2003. This package is a high-quality recording tool that features all the same bells and whistles as all the above programs, and is completely compatible with Adobe's video editing products: Adobe Premiere, Adobe After Effects, and Adobe Encore. Adobe products are for Windows only.

All of the programs listed above feature all the necessary basics of multitrack recording. They are all complete (and completely amazing) recording studio products created out of lines of computer code. They're all simply phenomenal products. The one that is right for you depends on a variety of factors, including:

1. **Your format**. Do you really want a DAW instead of a stand-alone recorder (with outboard effects to be purchased separately), or a studio-in-a-box (with built in effects, as described above)?

2. **Your price range**. You can spend as little as nothing (with the free downloads made available by most, if not all, of the above companies—though some of these are limited-time trial versions) or many, many thousands of dollars.

3. **Your current setup**. Is your Mac or PC pretty much obsolete? Older than two or three years puts it close. If so, add the cost of a new computer to the price of the above software. Or, do you have racks of outboard gear from your old analog recording system? If so, you might find it easier or more cost effective to choose a stand-alone recorder.

4. **Your needs**. Will eight tracks of audio be enough for you (now and later), or will you need 96? And will you need to record those 96 tracks simultaneously, or will you be overdubbing most of them? Will you be recording direct or miking guitar amps and other live instruments most of the time? Will you be doing a lot of MIDI work? Will you need to edit your recordings to a very fine degree, as in by the actual waveform and note by note, or won't you be sweating the fine details that much? Also, is there a certain piece of hardware (or even another piece of software, such as a loop editor or an effects processor plug-in) that your new system simply must be compatible with? (For more on loop editors, see tip #10; for more on plug-ins, see tip #11.) Do you need extremely high-resolution audio capabilities, such as 96 kHz (the standard for DVD audio), or will lesser resolution work for you?

I could go on, but I won't. Truthfully, there are so many things to think about, so many decisions to make. It really all comes down to each individual's situation, so making any specific recommendations here is beyond the scope of this book. Hopefully, however, you'll gather as much information as possible in order to properly match your needs with the best available product.

Get out there and talk to people about these issues. Visit stores and grill their top experts. Speak with other local musicians. Try to talk to engineers and recordists at a local pro recording studio and get their opinions. Search the Internet for manufacturer websites and related discussion forums. Read numerous books and magazines on the subject. Regardless of the frustration you will most certainly encounter with any DAW setup, I can guarantee you this: once you get up and running, you're going to have a blast!

10 RECORDING SOFTWARE, PART 2: LOOPS

Loops are building blocks with which you can actually create entire recordings—no live musicians required. Okay, that's not really fair; many of the best loop-sampler CDs feature recordings by some of the world's most incredible living, breathing musicians. What I meant was that you can use *those* recorded loops on *your* recording—royalty free—whether or not there is anyone living and breathing in your studio at all (although, hopefully, you are).

These days, there are hundreds—probably thousands—of phenomenal loop CDs available on the market, covering all musical genres and reproduced in all kinds of formats (audio, wav, mpg, etc.). Many loop packages focus on drums and percussion, although there are recorded sounds of virtually any instrument, voice, or sound effect imaginable, available in one-, two-, and four-measure patterns (among other options, such as individual "hits"). Just search for "loops" or "loop-based samples" on the Internet and you'll be amazed at the vast amount of products you'll find.

Want Aerosmith drummer Joey Kramer on your CD? Done. Want the Hammond organ player heard on recordings by Eric Clapton, Van Morrison, George Harrison, and others? Only a hundred bucks, and he's yours forever. Itching to have Motown stickmen Pistol Allen, Uriel Jones, and Jack Ashford laying down your grooves? No problem. If you can imagine hearing it on your recording, it's probably out there.

So what do you do with these loops once you have them in hand? Well, there are a number of very popular loop manipulation software packages on the market, with funny names such as Acid, Fruity Loops, and Plasma. And while these loop editing programs may seem complicated at first glance, to learn them is a largely intuitive process (meaning, you'll know basically what to do once you play around with the program). In many cases, manipulating loops with these programs is as simple as using the same computer commands you perform in your day job, i.e., copy/paste (control-c/control-v), cut (control-x), and undo (control-z), etc. Really, all you have to do is lay one loop end-to-end with another and build your song, measure by measure, loop by loop. Afterwards, you can either export that audio or file to a recording package like those discussed in tip #11, or to your stand-alone recorder or studio-in-a-box.

The differences between various loop software packages are mostly application-related: one may be better for a certain use than others. All of them can be considered the evolutionary progeny of MIDI sequencers. Most of them allow for click-and-drag type manipulation as well as changes in tempo without major hassle (a key element in matching loops). Most packages are simple to use, though they can all go long on features as your needs (and skills) grow. Programs are available for both Mac and PC. Some of the main programs that deserve your attention include:

- **ReCycle by Propellerhead Software** (http://www.propellerheads.se/). Available in both Mac and Windows formats, ReCycle 1.0, released in 1994, was the original loop editor. It's a popular program, but without multitrack functionality.

- **Acid Pro by Sonic Foundry (now a division of Sony Pictures)** (http://mediasoftware.sonypictures.com/). A Windows-based loop editor (and recording package), Acid Pro bested the abilities of ReCycle upon its release in 1998 by offering the same basic functions but in a multitrack format. Acid Pro allows for one-click previewing of any loop in your library, and automatically matches the tempos between your current project and your previews. You can even use Acid Pro to add audio to video projects. Acid Pro is easily the biggest seller of the loop editing programs discussed here.

- **Plasma by Cakewalk** (http://www.Cakewalk.com). This is a low-budget Windows-based offering that does have some slick features, such as allowing multiple files per track and alternate meters. Unfortunately, it doesn't have the auto-synced tempo feature in preview mode that Acid Pro has, among other things, but it's available at a fraction of Acid Pro's price.

- **Fruity-Loops by Image-Line Software** (http://www.fruityloops.com/). This is largely considered a dance music tool. A Windows-based program, Fruity-Loops contains plenty of its own sound-generators; but if you want to import loops off products you purchase elsewhere, you'll have to pay more money and install another Image-Line component called Zero-X BeatSlicer. But if you're into electronica, this is an essential tool.

- **Phrazer by BitHeadz** (http://www.BitHeadz.com). A Mac-based multitrack looper (which at one was time the only Mac-based multitrack looper), it's more or less an Acid Pro clone for Mac users. It's a bit lacking in ease of operation though: many of the main features are somewhat concealed, and some of the procedures require more than intuition to grasp. And Phrazer doesn't have many of the features the above programs provide, such as built-in MIDI sequencing (all the above programs in this section include MIDI sequencing capabilities).

- **Live by Ableton** (http://www.ableton.com/). Both a Mac and Windows program, it's the only multitrack loop editor offered for both platforms. Live was actually designed more for live performance than studio use—and as the use of onstage computers increases, this manufacturer may have this market cornered. Again, this program offers plenty of features, but MIDI sequencing is not one of them. Still, it could be the best choice if you're a Mac user.

So do you really need any of these programs, and can you deal with their learning curves? That's up to your musical goals. I use Acid Pro primarily to put together better-sounding (and more quickly created) drum tracks than I ever did with my old drum machines; then I bounce the finished rhythms over to my stand-alone hard disk recorder, where I then add live guitar, vocals, and other instruments. Many people use loop programs primarily for rhythm tracks—as evidenced by the plethora of drum loop CDs on the market—though, unlike me, they may opt to finish their entire recording within their computer.

It's possible that the software already in your arsenal might be able to handle some of the functions for which you'd otherwise rely on a loop editor. Most, if not all, loop editors are available through manufacturer websites in downloadable free-trial versions; if so, check them out thoroughly and at least scan the downloadable manuals. Also search the web for online discussion forums pertaining to these software packages, and heed their advice before laying down any cash.

11 RECORDING SOFTWARE, PART 3:
PLUG-INS AND EVERYTHING ELSE

Even if your actual DAW recording software comes fully loaded with all the cool effects processors you could ever imagine, it's likely that you'll eventually want to incorporate plug-ins and other add-ons. Plug-ins are additional software programs that include everything from effects processors to soft-synths (software synthesizers) to drum machines to amp modelers to a few things that haven't even been invented yet.

Many of the top studio effects processors, which for decades have been used for in pro studios in their original hardware configurations, are now available in software plug-in versions. And even though plug-ins are devoid of a processor's metal chassis and extensive electronic circuitry, they aren't necessarily any cheaper. So, if you've long hungered for a Teletronix LA-2A or UA 1176 compressor/limiter, but have moved into the digital recording realm and are done with housing racks full of hardware, you're in luck: those two classic devices are now available as software plug-ins, as are hundreds of other new and legendary processors.

Such is the case for more than processors. As mentioned above, you can also set up your virtual studio with plug-in synthesizers, drum machines, guitar amp and speaker cabinet modelers, and much more. Steve Vai raves about a plug-in called SoundReplacer, with which he replaced weak bass drum hits on his live recordings of his European tour (and which later surfaced on his *Alive in an Ultra World* CD.

But there is a catch: not all plug-ins are compatible on all DAW recording software. There are many plug-in formats, including MIDI, VST (Virtual Studio Technology), MAS (MOTU Audio System), RTAS (Real Time Audio Suite), TDM (Time Division Multiplexing), HTDM (Host Time Division Multiplexing), Audio Suite, DXi (DirectX technology), and ReWire, to name a few of the most popular. No one recording program accepts all plug-ins, and some studio software manufacturers, such as Emagic, support only proprietary plug-ins—a factor to consider carefully before making a final decision on the recording studio software you'll install in your computer.

12 POWER IT UP CORRECTLY

No one ever thinks of this stuff, do they?

- **AC Power Cords**. In case you still aren't sure, yes, the same heavy power cord that runs your home computer will run your Marshall amp or most any other serious music-related electrical device—including high-end digital recording decks. Don't lose you day job stealing computer power cords from your employer; they only cost a few bucks at places like Home Depot or Radio Shack.

    When substituting power cords, just make sure you don't use something too skimpy, or you might have a meltdown—probably in the cord, but possibly in your electronic device (Hey, I'm not responsible for your failed electrical experiments!). And don't defeat the benefit of the three-prong grounded plug ends by using adapters if you can help it—and certainly don't ever permanently alter the plug. Doing so will only add noise to the system, and could increase your risk of fire or electrical shock (Oh, and don't use your high-end recording devices while bathing, showering, or swimming either; the smell of burnt flesh rarely incites great performances).

- **Extension Cords and Power Strips**. Use heavy-duty—not typical household—extension cords and power strips whenever possible. You'll likely be running a lot of current through these things, especially if you've got a recorder, mixer, outboard effects, and guitar amps all plugged in simultaneously. And try to spread the power draw around to several—if not completely, separately fused—wall outlets, too, whenever possible.

- **Surge Protectors**. If you think you need a surge protector, you do. Don't risk losing all your hard work during an electrical storm or freak power outage. Plug all your computer and digital devices into surge protectors.

- **Lights and Other Useless Electricity Hogs**. Candles probably aren't a good idea, but try to keep your lighting on a different circuit from your recording gear, if possible. Lights, air conditioners, television sets, refrigerators, electric-powered hookahs—they all create magnetic interference that can diminish the quality of your recordings, not to mention occasional electrical surges (air conditioners especially), which could downright ruin your recording. Turn everything off that you don't absolutely need, and isolate everything else from your recording and musical gear as much as possible.

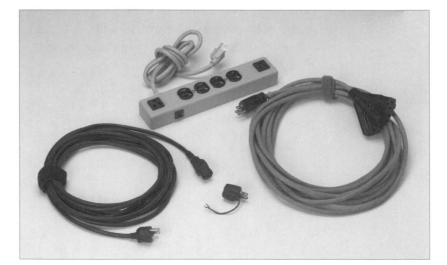

13 CAREFUL WITH THE CONDENSER

Don't ruin your expensive condenser microphones by using them to record loud guitars or the inside of a bass drum. Condenser mics are fragile and easily ruined by high sound pressure level. If you're determined to use a condenser mic to record your screaming, 100 watt Marshall amp, you may find that the microphone is no longer useful for its true purpose—recording vocals, acoustic guitars, and other non-amplified instruments—and that you'll then have relegated it to use *only* on loud instruments.

14 GET A FEW EXTRA LONG CABLES

In a small home studio, you might occasionally find it necessary to place a loud sound source—such as a blaring guitar speaker cabinet or drum set—in another room, far from your "control room." In the case of a guitarist, for example, you could have the player and his or her amp head and effects pedals or rack in the control room, with a long speaker cable running into another room where the speaker cabinet is blasting out at un-Godly volumes. Actually, this is done all the time, even in the biggest pro studios. Pete Anderson, Dwight Yoakam's producer and lead guitarist, has mentioned that he does this routinely, especially when recording solos and "sweeteners."

You can then run extra long mic cables out of there, too—like down the hall to your nice, 'verby bathroom, basement, or garage—where the room mics will pick up better ambient sounds off the amp than in the confines of a small, dead-sounding room (like your converted bedroom-turned-recording-studio?). This will drastically speed the process of tracking and overdubbing, since the guitarist and engineer (might they both be you?) can then operate in a normal conversational manner, despite the racket the cabinet is putting out.

Of course you'll have to use the correct cables for the job. Speaker cables are specially designed to run from a power source (such as a guitar amp) to a speaker cabinet. Guitar cables are not suitable for this purpose, and will degrade the tonal characteristics of the amp. If you're going to separate the amp head and speaker cabinet for any reason, you'll be limited by the length of speaker cable you have. This might mean that you have to buy an extra speaker cable, say a 25- or even 50-footer, to have around your studio, just in case. If you're miking a drummer in this way, or if the guitarist wants to stand out there next to the cabinet for better guitar pickup/speaker cabinet interaction, you'll also need an extra long headphone cable(s). You might rarely need to set up this way, or you might find yourself doing it all the time. Either way, it'll be well worth a few extra dollars in cables in the final product.

15 CORDS AND CONNECTORS

We've all got to deal with them, regardless of our studio setup. No, I'm not talking about significant others; I'm talking about cords and connectors. It may seem obvious, but you've always got to make sure you're using the right cord and connector for the job at hand. Here are a few sage words of advice directly from my wife, a big music fan: "Just because you can plug it in doesn't mean it belongs there." Okay, right dear. Good advice. We'll be sure to keep that in mind.

- **The ¼-Inch Analog Plug**. An analog cord with a ¼-inch plug is the most common cord/connector used by musicians; it's the one used by all electric guitarists and most keyboardists. But ¼-inch plugs actually come in two varieties: mono/TS (tip/sleeve) and stereo/TRS (tip/ring/sleeve). In addition, two cords, both with ¼-inch TS connectors, may be wired differently, depending on whether their intended use is as an instrument or speaker cable. Take care that you're using the correct ¼-inch cable for your application.

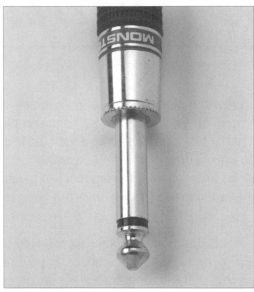

mono/TS 1/4-inch plug

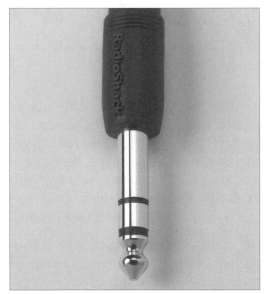

stereo/TRS 1/4-inch plug

- **Mono/TS Instrument Cords**. Inside an *instrument* TS cord is a wire connected to the metal tip of the connector. The sleeve of the connector—the rest of the metal part—is separated from the tip by a plastic divider. The wire inside the cord is wrapped inside a braided wire "shield," which blocks noise from interfering with the signal carried on the wire within. This shield is connected to the sleeve of the connector. A tip/sleeve cord has only one channel—one wire— through which to send signal, i.e., it is only capable of carrying a mono signal. Instrument cords are sometimes referred to as "unbalanced" or "high-impedance" cords. (See TRS cords for an explanation of "balanced" cords.)

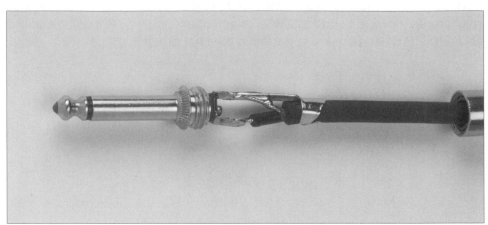

mono/TS instrument cord

- **Mono/TS Speaker Cords**. Inside a *speaker* TS cord are two wires: one connected to the metal tip of the connector, the other connected to the sleeve. The sleeve is still separated from the tip by a plastic divider, but the wire inside a speaker cord has no shield, so there's room for two wires to be run through instead. The wires inside the speaker cord are capable of carrying much more power, or "current," than the wire inside an instrument cable (they're usually a heavier gauge wire). This increased current blocks most interfering noise; that's why no is shield is required. Don't plug an instrument with a speaker cord, or you'll get noise or even radio interference on the unshielded line.

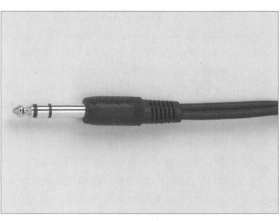

mono/TS speaker cord

- **Stereo/TRS Cords**. A stereo headphone cable with a ¼-inch plug is an example of a stereo/TRS cord. Inside a stereo/TRS cord are two wires: one connected to the metal tip of the connector, the other to the ring. These two wires are shielded by a braided wire wrapping, which is connected to the sleeve. The tip, ring, and sleeve are all separated by plastic dividers. This type of cord is also called "balanced" or "low impedance."

A balanced cord is one with the same signal running through both wires, but one signal at 180 degrees out of phase with the other. The idea is that any noise waveforms picked up by the cord will be mirror images of themselves while out of phase. When the signal gets through the cord to its destination, such as into your recording deck, the deck will flip one of the signals so that both are in phase; then the mirror image noise waveforms will cancel each other out, while the "good" signal waveforms will boost themselves into one, much stronger signal.

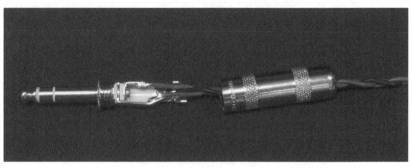

stereo/TRS cord

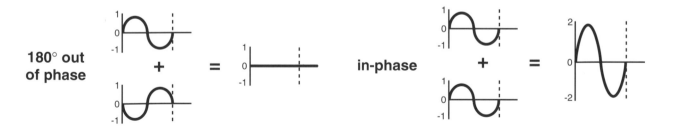

Balanced cords are typically used to connect professional components together—such as your mixing board and recording deck. The advantage of balanced cords over unbalanced cords is that they can be run in longer lengths without increased noise.

- **Stereo/TRS Y Cords**. A Y cord looks like the letter "Y." It's got a stereo/TRS plug on one end, and two mono/TS plugs on the other ends. A Y cord is wired so that the tip of the TRS plug sends a signal, while the ring of the TRS plug receives the return signal. The sleeve is connected to a braided wire shield. The Y cord is used to insert an outboard device—such as a compressor, equalizer, or effects unit—into a line-in, insert, or effects send/return jack of a mixer or recording deck (or other pro device). Insert the TRS plug into your mixer or deck—one TS

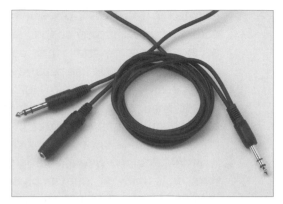

plug into the "in" jack of the outboard device, and the other TS plug into the "out" jack of the outboard device. That's it. Done.

- **The XLR Analog Plug**. The XLR connector is your basic microphone plug, which you'll most often use with microphones, although you will sometimes use an XLR-equipped mic cable to connect two pro audio devices. XLRs are balanced, low-impedance (or low-Z, as they are sometimes called) cords, wired much like a stereo/TRS cord but with a different format connector on the end. Some lower-priced recording decks and mixers do not accept XLR cables. If this is the case in your studio, your equipment might be high-impedance; in which case, you'll

want to get a low- to high-impedance transformer (expect to spend around $20; more for higher quality models). Not all XLR-to-$\frac{1}{4}$-inch TRS adapter plugs function as transformers—it may be an adapter exclusively, which may not suit your purposes.

- **The RCA Plug**. RCA plugs are also called "phono" plugs because they've been in common use for generations with our home stereos (once known, back in the dark ages, as "phonographs"). They are the little plugs with the sharp metal ring around the male tip, which allows them to be used in both analog and digital capacities. RCA plug-equipped cords are similar to mono/TS cords, though they can be used in a digital capacity for S/PDIF signals as well. There is a difference, however, between a basic RCA-tipped audio cord and an RCA-tipped

digital audio cord: RCA audio cords will allow sound degradation when stretched beyond three or four feet. If you need to run a longer RCA cord, buy digital audio, or even video, cords instead of regular audio cords.

- **The Mini Plug**. Mini plugs are sometimes confused with RCA plugs, but they have a much more finished look to them. They're simply a tiny little analog audio connector of the sort usually featured on low-end headphones and inexpensive consumer audio gear. They come in mono and stereo versions (wired similarly to mono/TS and stereo/TRS cables, respectively). There are many adapters to go from $\frac{1}{4}$-inch to mini and back, as well as to XLR, and just about everything else.

- **Digital Cords and Connectors**. Other digital cords or connectors, besides the RCAs, include MIDI, non-RCA types of S/PDIF (such as fiber-optic cables with Toslink connectors), AES/EBU, ADAT Lightpipe, TDIF, and SCSI. Some cords and connectors, particularly digital and/or fiber-optic kinds, can be quite expensive. Don't forget to budget for the proper cabling in your studio or you may find yourself staring at a bunch of beautiful but silent toys until your wife hands over your next semi-annual allowance.

- **MIDI Cords**. MIDI, which stands for Musical Instrument Digital Interface, is simply a communication protocol that allows information to pass between devices. Although largely associated with keyboards and sequencers, MIDI is applicable to almost any instrument, effects processor, or recording deck these days. MIDI cords have five-pin male connectors on each end that plug into the female MIDI jack built into every MIDI instrument or device. If you have several MIDI devices, you'll need several MIDI cables.

- **S/PDIF Cords**. This funny acronym, pronounced "spuh-diff," stands for Sony/Phillips Digital Interface Format. S/PDIF cords are typically unbalanced coaxial cable, with one wire and a shield (similar to TS wires) and RCA connectors on both ends. They also come constructed with fiber-optic cable and a Toslink connector, which is a small, square plug. S/PDIF can simultaneously transmit two channels of digital data.

- **AES/EBU Cords**. Cords and connectors built to the exacting specifications of the Audio Engineering Society/European Broadcasting Union are referred to as AES/EBU cables. They're similar to S/PDIF cords, but they're built using XLR connectors and balanced cords (similar to stereo/TRS cords) for higher quality transmission.

- **ADAT Lightpipe Cords**. Alesis designed this fiber-optic cord with special connector to transmit up to eight tracks of digital audio at one time; then they allowed other manufacturers to use their technology. This helped to make the ADAT Lightpipe cable and connector a standard digital audio product.

- **TDIF Connectors**. Teac followed Alesis's Lightpipe lead by attaching their 25-pin connector to a standard computer cable, also capable of simultaneously transmitting up to eight digital audio signals.

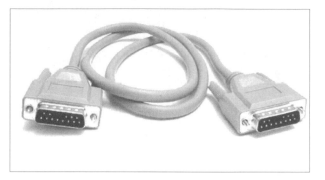

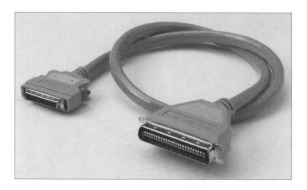

- **SCSI Cables**. Many computer users are familiar with the SCSI cable from their boring, old day jobs. SCSI came into many others' lives when they purchased external CD burners for their recording decks. SCSI cables and connectors can be fairly expensive. Also, they're quite stiff and can't be run too long; so plan their placement and routing accordingly. And don't forget to acquire a SCSI terminator if your end-of-the-line SCSI device doesn't have an internal terminator (and it probably doesn't if it has two SCSI ports—in which case, one would be "In," the other would be "Thru"; similar to MIDI In and MIDI Out/Thru.)

- **USB Cables**. The Universal Serial Bus, or USB cable/connector, is another familiar item to most contemporary computer users. USB is a fast way to transmit data, and many high-end audio products support USB technology. These cables are fairly inexpensive.

One more thing about cords and connectors: you get what you pay for. Cheap cords and connectors allow for more noise and are likely to break sooner. They're not sexy purchases, but try not to skimp on quality with your cords and connectors.

16 THAT'S NOT MY GUITAR SOUND

If your recorded guitar has more distortion and bass than you heard coming from the amp, it's probably because your microphone is closer to the speaker(s) than your ears, causing the mic to pick up more distortion and bottom end. Most electric guitars are recorded with one mic placed up close, and at least one room mic placed so as to capture a more ambient sound (a sound more similar to what the player hears).

Late producer Tom Dowd, who recorded Eric Clapton, Lynyrd Skynyrd, the Allman Brothers Band, and many other greats, told me specifically that, in addition to placing a mic close against the amp's grill cloth, he would almost always place another mic about a foot away from the amp, facing up or across axis. This second mic would capture the full wave of the low end, and would also absorb the color the closer mic wasn't picking up. Mixed together, the sounds from these two mics would more closely portray what Duane Allman, Dickey Betts, or Eric Clapton heard when they played, which was ultimately what they wanted to hear recorded.

In addition to following Dowd's suggestion, you might try placing a room mic at or near ear level and about five or six feet away from the amp. This mic should blend in well with your close mic, probably making your guitarist happier with the recorded tone. Of course, the level on this far mic will be lower, so it may need some boost and compression. To capture a broader frequency range that more closely matches the full spectrum of human hearing, use a condenser mic (which is better suited for this situation than a dynamic mic). Also, when you've placed a microphone far away from the amp like this, you might need to boost your bass EQ on either the amp or the board to make up for the loss in bass proximity caused by the distance. For more on bass proximity, see tip #18.

TRACK 1

17 MICROPHONES EXPLAINED

There are basically three types of microphones that you'll encounter or use in a recording situation: dynamic, condenser, and ribbon. Here are simple explanations of each, including their main uses and some of their pros and cons:

Dynamic microphones: such as a Shure SM58 or Audix OM-6, are pressure-operated, electro-magnetic devices. When sound waves exert pressure on a diaphragm located inside the microphone, a coil attached to the diaphragm moves, disrupting a magnetic field. From this movement and disruption an electronic signal is created.

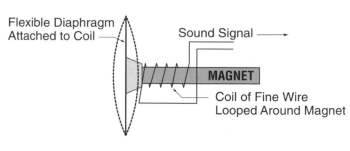

Moving Coil Microphone

Dynamic mics can be designed to be either *(uni)directional* or *omnidirectional*. Directional mics are sensitive only to sound coming from a single direction; omnidirectional mics are sensitive to sound coming from all directions.

The most common directional, or pickup, pattern is called *cardioid*, and refers to the mic's ability to pick up sounds from a source in front while largely rejecting sounds from the sides and back. The diagram of a cardioid microphone's response-to-sound-source pattern extends 360 degrees around the mic in a somewhat heart-like (hence the name cardioid) shape. These mics can also be *hyper-cardioid* and *supercardioid*, which means that their pickup patterns allow for slightly more sound to be received from "off axis" (mostly behind the mic) sources than does a cardioid mic. (See tip #19.)

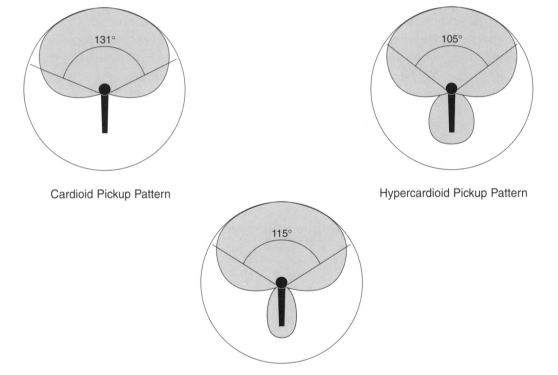

Cardioid Pickup Pattern

Hypercardioid Pickup Pattern

Supercardioid Pickup Pattern

Dynamic mics are often used in live concert vocal applications, though top engineers will usually place a high-end condenser mic in front of a singer during a recording session. Late producer Tom Dowd (Allman Brothers, Derek and the Dominos) told me that he considered the directional, super-cardioid Shure SM57 to be the standard for miking guitar amps or snare drums, both live and in the studio, due mainly to its ability to handle high sound pressure levels (SPL). History would suggest that most engineers have agreed with Dowd. Dynamic mics are also usually built to be quite rugged, so they can take a little knocking around; plus they're inexpensive compared to ribbon and condenser mics.

On the negative side, while dynamic mics can stand high SPLs without distorting—or tearing themselves to shreds—they often do not have a full frequency range. The SM57, for instance, has a frequency response of 40 Hz to 15 kHz, with a peak in the 2.5 to 6 kHz range. For this reason, it probably shouldn't be your first choice for instruments rich in higher harmonics, such as violin or chimes.

Condenser microphones: such as the Shure SM81, vintage Neumann U47, the Telefunken Ela M 251, or the Audix SCX-25 employ *electrostatic* means to capture sounds (as opposed to the electromagnetic technology used by dynamic and ribbon microphones). There is no magnet in a condenser microphone; instead, a pressure-sensitive capacitor (an electronic part formerly known as a "condenser," hence the microphone's name), reacts to the sound pressure reaching the mic, creating an electrical signal.

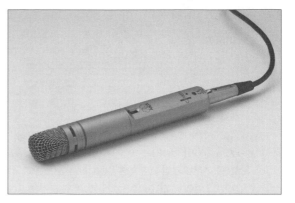

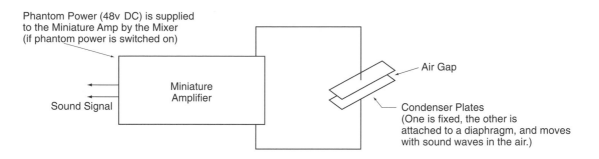

Because they are pressure sensitive, condenser mics are omnidirectional. Condenser mics are often designed so that their pickup patterns can be changed—from omnidirectional to cardioid to *bidirectional*, or *figure eight*. Condenser mics are treasured for their clarity and great sensitivity, as well as for their ability to capture a wide range of frequencies.

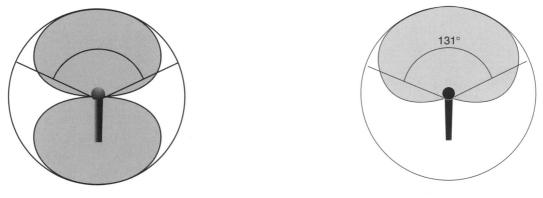

Figure 8 Pattern   Cardioid Pattern

Condensers are generally used on acoustic instruments where sound quality and tone are extremely important—characteristics that are sometimes difficult to capture with a less sensitive (read: dynamic) microphone. They are also excellent mics for recording vocal tracks. You'll often hear condenser mics (and sometimes dynamic mics as well) characterized as large- or small-diaphragm. Large-diaphragm condensers are often used when a warm, low-end is desired, and is also the perfect choice for an acoustic or standup bass. Small-diaphragm condenser mics are better at capturing high-frequency sounds, such as cymbals and other small percussion instruments, and even acoustic guitars.

Condenser mics usually need their own "phantom" power source—a dedicated power supply or the mixing board. Some condensers operate on batteries. (It's also worth mentioning that a certain breed of condenser mics—known as "electret" condensers—still requires power, but uses it in a slightly different manner. But since the end result is the same, I'll not elaborate on that difference here).

The often-expensive condenser mics are indeed sensitive, and therefore can easily be driven to distortion. In fact, they can actually be ruined by high sound pressure levels. They're fragile too; dropping one could spell its demise. Despite these drawbacks, there is nothing like using a quality condenser or two on an acoustic guitar in a nice-sounding room. Every studio should have at least one.

Ribbon microphones: such as the Royer SF-12, Royer R-121, Coles 4038, or BeyerDynamic M260 are also known as pressure-gradient or velocity mics. Ribbon microphones get their name from the thin metal ribbon suspended between the poles of a magnet inside the mic. When sound waves move the ribbon, voltage is created in the ribbon. That voltage then becomes the electronic signal output.

Ribbon mics are primarily bidirectional, which means that they receive sound waves from both the front and rear, creating a figure-eight-shaped pickup pattern. Sound waves coming toward the sides of the ribbon microphone cancel each other out. However, like condensers, ribbon mics are often designed so that their pickup patterns can be switched from figure eight to cardioid and even to omnidirectional—this occurs when ports at the back of the microphone are closed off, preventing the signal from coming into the microphone from the back.

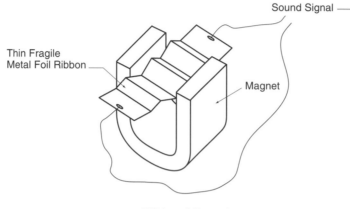

Sound Signal ⟶

Thin Fragile
Metal Foil Ribbon

Magnet

Ribbon Microphone

Top producers and engineers such as Steve Albini (Nirvana, Cheap Trick), Eddie Kramer (Jimi Hendrix, Kiss, Led Zeppelin), and Ed Cherney (Rolling Stones, Eric Clapton) swear by ribbon microphones for guitars, basses, drums, and all kinds of sound sources. The natural warmth of a ribbon microphone is renowned, with some saying it brings back a little analog sound to our overly digital world. Carlos Santana even uses one to mic his amp when playing live. Ribbon mics are a popular choice for engineers recording horns and vocals—again, for their warmth.

Alas, the downside to ribbon mics is that they are very expensive and can be quite fragile—high SPLs can blow out the delicate ribbon. So if you do pony up $1,000 or more for one, be careful when placing it close to a loud sound source. Beware that it costs about $125 to replace a ribbon—more than the total cost of a Shure SM-58. Also, like condenser mics, many ribbon mics require "phantom" power—meaning they need their own power source in order to operate. This is an extra consideration (and expense) you should discuss with your local microphone expert before making an investment in a ribbon mic. Fortunately, some mixing boards and other outboard gear are capable of serving as a power source for such microphones; so depending on what gear you're using in your studio setup, you may not need to purchase an additional power source.

TRACK 2

18 BASS PROXIMITY EFFECT

The closer you put a microphone to your sound source—including your lips when singing live or recording vocals—the more audio from the bass end of the spectrum the microphone will pick up. This increase in bass is pickup is known as the "bass proximity effect"; and it can have a substantial effect on your recorded sound. For instance, the mic I use for my live lead vocals is a Shure Beta SM58A, which is an upgraded version of Shure's classic SM58. The specs on this mic point out that placing the mic one-eighth of an inch from the sound source (as when I press my lips right up against the mic while singing) can increase the bass response by as much as 17 dB more than if I were standing two feet away from the mike (that is, up to a 17 dB increase on the lowest bass frequencies I produce; equivalent to the first few notes on my bass player's low E string).

This is a *considerable* bass boost, and could seriously affect the overall EQ of my recordings (not to mention that it could drive my live engineer boffo). Even the final couple of inches make a big difference: the specs on my Beta 58A show that the bass response can increase by approximately 5 dB if the mic is moved from two inches to one inch from the sound source, and another 5 dB if moved from one inch to one-eighth of an inch. And it's not just my mic that does this; all microphones react this way.

Those annoying "booms" and "pops" will be especially pronounced if you don't adjust for the bass proximity effect—and will be even more of a problem if you're not using a pop filter (see tip #21). Basically, just back off from the mic a little and you'll avoid this dilemma. Of course, if you're recording guitar tracks and you want to get the heavy low end so popular in today's rock recordings, you can add that low end by placing the mic within this extra bass zone. The choice is yours.

TRACK 2

19 ON- AND OFF-AXIS MICS

The phrases "on-axis" and "off-axis" refer to the imaginary lines that run either through the middle of the microphone, parallel to the microphone, or perpendicular to its diaphragm (imagine a dynamic mic for this example). On-axis refers to a mic pointing straight at the sound source. Off-axis refers to a mic whose sound source is at the back or to the sides. For example, a mic placed 90 degrees off-axis is completely perpendicular to the sound source; one placed 180 degrees off-axis has its grill facing directly away from the sound source. A knowledge of these terms will help you to better understand a mic's pickup pattern, as well as any tips you pick up (either from this book or elsewhere) that refer to off-axis mic placement.

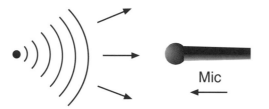

Sound Source

on-axis mic placement

Sound Source

off-axis mic placement (90 degrees)

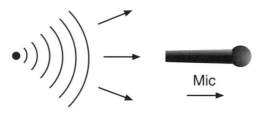

Sound Source

off-axis mic placement (180 degrees)

For example, legendary producer Tom Dowd once told me that he would often place mics as much as 90 degrees off-axis in the studio—particularly the bass drum mic. Dowd, who before his 2002 death produced most of the classic albums by the Allman Brothers Band, as well as significant recordings by hundreds of other stars and legends, explained that by positioning the mic 90 degrees off-axis (sideways to the sound source), it would still pick up plenty of signal, but would be spared the overwhelming air movement that often leads to distortion or excessive bass proximity effect. Try this 90-degree (or up to 90-degree) off-axis placement on your own kick drum, bass speaker cabinet, or guitar speakers—even your vocals—and see if you don't prefer the results over regular on-axis miking.

TRACK 2

20 ELIMINATING PHASE PROBLEMS

Let's say that, in addition to a close mic, you used a room mic to capture your combo guitar amp, live drum kit, or gold-plated baby grand; and the recording sounds weak and "hollow." You've got a phase problem. But no need to worry; this is an easy problem to fix. You just need to learn a little bit about phase and phase cancellation.

Sound waves, as from a musical instrument or other sound source, are said to be in "phase" when their waveforms are synchronous. As with waves in water, sound waves have peaks and valleys, or crests and troughs. When you place two microphones in position to record a combo guitar amp, for example, each mic will capture its own version of those sound waves. If the sound wave sets captured by each of the two mics hit their crests and troughs simultaneously, or are in phase, the waves captured "combine" to create a bigger sound than either mic would have captured alone. However, if the mics are placed in such a way that the crests and troughs of the sound wave are not aligned, the two signals being captured by the two mics will start to cancel each other out, degrading the final recorded sound. This is known as "phase cancellation."

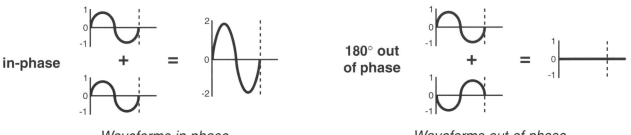

Waveforms in phase   *Waveforms out of phase*

Phase cancellation can be a desired effect—for example, the ethereal sounds that come out of the guitar effect pedal known as a flanger. You always have the option to allow some degree of phase cancellation—even going so far as to cause it intentionally—if you think that it adds a cool texture to your recording.

However, phase cancellation is usually avoided, as it can cause a your recordings to sound "hollow," lacking punch and definition within certain frequencies. This is often the result of placing a room mic at some distance from a sound source. Just like our two-mic example above, a room mic's placement causes it to pick up (at least) two sets of sound waves: those that come directly from the sound source, and those that come from the sound bouncing off the floor, walls, or any nearby reflective surface. Because these reflected sounds are slightly delayed on their way to the microphone (they traveled an indirect route to get there), the combination of the direct and indirect sound waves will result in some degree of phase cancellation. Fortunately, there are things you can do to minimize the damage.

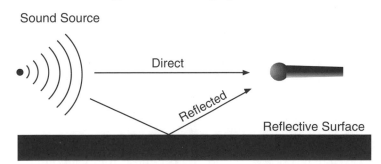

First, try moving your room mic closer to the floor, wall, or reflecting surface—as close as an inch or less. Placing your microphone less than one-eighth of an inch from the reflecting surface will increase the frequency of phase cancellation, but only above 10 kHz—where it won't be as noticeable. Also, you'll get an increase of as much as 6 dB in the output of the mic. Of course, you can also reduce the intensity of any reflected sounds by using absorptive materials, such as carpeting, curtains, or baffles; which will combat the phase cancellation captured by room mics.

TRACK 3

 21 NYLONS AND LOLLIPOPS:
THE MAKING OF A POP FILTER

No, a pop filter isn't going to reduce your ability to record a hit pop song! Pop filters help to remove those annoying "pop" sounds that occur naturally whenever a singer articulates the letters "p" or "b," and a few other letters too (and by overwhelming the vocal mic with a blast of their whiskey-freshened breath). You can go out and buy a pop filter—but wouldn't it be more fun to make your own? (Especially since it requires that you go down to the store to buy a nice fresh pair of nylon stockings; I like the ones with the seam up the back, but you can choose whatever tickles your fancy).

All kidding aside, that's right: go get yourself a pair of nylons, and a wire coat hanger, too. Bend the coat hanger into a circle about six to eight inches across, with the remaining wire left hanging down—the finished product should look like a big lollipop on a stick. (Nylons and lollipops! Hey, this book is getting better fast!)

Now stretch the toe of the stocking over the circle of wire, then knot and cut away the excess. Voila! A pop filter. You can attach your new pop filter to your mic stand by twining the hanging wire around the stand, then duct-taping it into place. (Don't do this to the mic stand you're going to take to a live performance; you'll get some awfully strange looks.)

Now position the pop filter about two inches in front of your microphone, directly between the mic and the singer. The vocalist's lips should be at least a couple inches from the filter. If the vocalist seems to be drawn to the nylons—sort of like a wino to an alley—first assure him or her that the nylons were never worn, then move the filter another couple inches away from the mic. There—no more poppy vocal tracks. Well, unless you're… uh… never mind.

TRACK 2

22 SMILE WHEN YOU SAY THAT, SON

There's another way to defeat the pop; and while it doesn't require any unusual purchases at your local grocery store, it does require some practice. The late producer Tom Dowd told me that he often asked his vocalists (and remember: he recorded everyone from Ray Charles to Aretha Franklin to Rod Stewart to Gregg Allman) to sing with smiles on their faces. Literally, smiles.

Smiling while singing actually reduces a vocalist's ability to pop a puff of air toward the microphone—even when mouthing the usual culprits: words like "baby," "body," and "please" (uh… I mean words with "b"s and "p"s). Dowd demonstrated his technique to by holding a lit match in front of my mouth. When I wasn't smiling, the word "baby" blew the match out. When I was smiling, I couldn't blow out the match, no matter how I tried. (Not to say I could actually sing either, but that's not important here.)

If a certain application requires a directional mic (i.e., to isolate a sound source when other sounds are bleeding into your mic), but instead of a cardioid mic you have a couple of other kinds of mics on hand, you're still in luck. You can mimic the pickup pattern of a cardioid mic by using an omnidirectional and bidirectional mic together on the sound source. Use whichever combination of condenser (electrostatic) mics and dynamic or ribbon (electromagnetic) mics to create this effect.

Place the omnidirectional and the bidirectional mics on-axis, as physically close to each other as possible, and as close to the sound source as required. Run each mic to its own board channel. Now, if both mic levels are set the same (and the mics are equally sensitive), the resulting mix of the two mics should be equivalent to that of one cardioid mic.

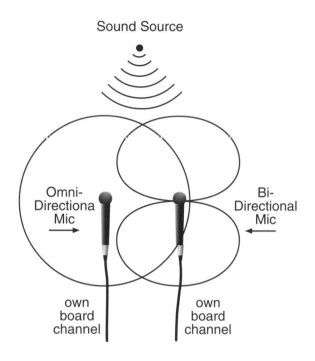

By raising the level of the omnidirectional mic, you'll increase the signal captured at 90 degrees off-axis, which will push the pickup pattern toward omnidirectional. By raising the level of the bidirectional mic, you will increase the signal captured at 180 degrees off axis, which will push the pickup pattern toward figure eight. With the mic levels balanced on the board, the signal coming from off-axis will be out of phase between the two mics, and thus will largely cancel out; while the on-axis signal coming from both mics will be in phase, and twice as powerful as the off-axis signal—creating a cardioid pattern.

By using this setup, and varying the level of the omnidirectional mic from zero to full, any directional pattern can be created: from figure eight to cardioid to omni-directional. Experiment with different settings and see what sounds good in your situation.

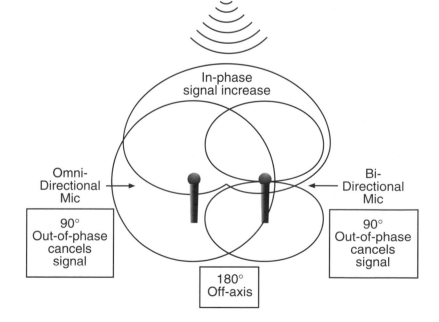

24 CLOSE YOUR EYES AND LISTEN

Most of us use our eyes to get around, play an instrument, or set up a microphone. As such, you'll encounter in a thousand different places, including this book, the rule for the optimal positioning of a microphone on a guitar speaker cabinet (approximately 2 o'clock, facing slightly toward the cone of the speaker)—which is clearly a visual reference. But music is not a visual medium; it's an aural one. So why do we rely on our eyes to determine optimal mic placement?

But that guideline is meant only to get you in the ballpark of the oft-discussed, mic placement "sweet spot." To lock it in—to get the microphone positioned in exactly the location where it can best capture the perfect tone of the instrument—you must use your ears. Close your eyes, and listen. Learn to hear how a subtle change in the position of the mic can make a huge tonal difference in the sound.

Once you find the microphone's sweet spot (and every situation, not to mention every microphone, will be different), don't change the position of the mic after opening your eyes again and visually deciding that it "can't possibly be right." Often, the sweet spot will jump out in an off-axis microphone position; don't be surprised by this, and don't discount the results based on visual cues alone. And just like everything else in life, practice will enhance your listening skill.

25 DISTANCE = DEPTH

When you're singing into a microphone, the distance you put between your lips and the microphone affects the "depth" of your recording, in a three-dimensional kind of way. Want to sound like you're screaming in someone's ear from point-blank range? Get right on the mic. Want a little roomier ambience to the track? Back off a few inches. These mere few inches make a world of difference in the tone and level that a microphone will pick up.

As mentioned before, the issue of placement distance—whether it's you as vocalist placing your lips a certain distance from the microphone, or you as engineer placing the microphone a certain distance from a guitar amp or other sound source—is directly correlated to the three-dimensional-like depth captured in your recordings, and which you can control almost as easily as you control panning left and right. Listen to the recordings of a symphony orchestra and soak up the ambient sound—the front-to-back "picture" you get from the recording. This effect is largely the result of microphone positioning (though some of this effect can be achieved in the mix as well).

TRACK 2

26 NATURAL CONDENSATION

When using a condenser mic, don't allow the sound source to be right on top of the microphone. Back off from the mic a little and turn the input trim up a little on the mixer or recorder. This adds a natural compression and a bit of reverb or room ambience to your signal, without the use of compressors or reverb units. Also, to fix a thin sound, instead of playing around with the EQ on the board, change the position of the microphone to slightly off-axis. This will cut the highs and boost the mids a little, thickening the sound.

TRACK 4

Until his death in 2002, legendary record producer Tom Dowd, whose career spanned six decades, recorded thousands of albums by everyone from the Allman Brothers to Eric Clapton to Ray Charles and Aretha Franklin. Dowd was a champion of off-axis microphone use, as noted elsewhere in this book. He told me that one of his favorite techniques for miking guitar amps—and specifically to mike the Allman Brothers' Dickey Betts's guitars—was to put one microphone straight into the speaker, as close as possible; usually touching the grill cloth. Dowd preferred the mic to be on-axis and pointed directly at the center of the speaker cone.

Dowd would then place another microphone six inches (or more) back, and as much as 90 degrees off axis. He would then change the position of this mic as needed to eliminate phase cancellation (Dowd suggested checking for phase cancellation between the mics in mono). The result: changing the axis of the backup microphone added variations to the EQ coloring captured by this mic. Therefore, the mix of the two mics together provided broader sonic possibilities.

TRACK 5

28 AUDIO AND POWER CORDS

Don't run your audio cables too close to your AC power lines, as they'll pick up magnetic interference, which of course translates as noise to your recorder. If you must lay out an audio cable near an AC line, don't run them parallel to each other: again the audio cable will pick up noise. Run the audio cable across the AC power line at a perpendicular angle.

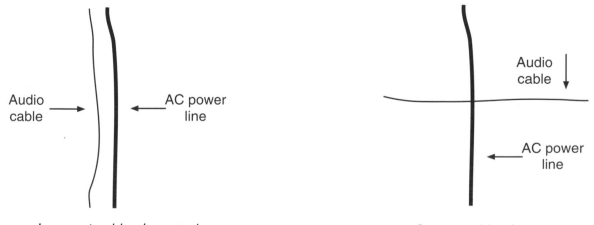

| *Incorrect cable placement* | *Correct cable placement* |

Also, never coil lengthy AC or audio cables—these coils, such as the slack in a long extension cord, will create a magnetic field that may interfere with your instruments (especially a single-coil guitar pickup) or recording devices. Coiled audio cables are just noise traps waiting for some hapless electromagnetism to fly by.

29 IT'S BAFFLING

Baffles are usually put into play in large studios for live band recordings, but they can also come in handy for the home recording enthusiast who simply doesn't want to blast the neighbors into calling the police.

If you need some easy-to-move, easy-to-store baffles, just drape a large, heavy blanket or old curtain over a sheet of plywood, a few extra guitar or mic stands, a couple of music stands, or anything else that can sustain the material and support its weight.

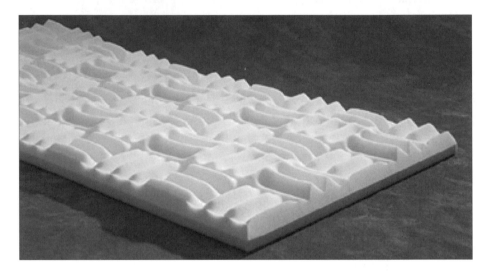

Or you can get a little more elaborate and build yourself some simple baffles. Just staple sheets of cotton baffling to plywood (attach 2 x 4s for the feet), then cover the baffling with a grill-cloth-type fabric. You can probably get the baffling and grill cloth from your local fabric store; if they don't have these items, they'll at least be able to tell you where they are available.

30 MAKESHIFT ISOLATION BOOTH

You can create a makeshift recording "booth" for your guitar amp with some baffles placed in a closet or under a table or desk. Doing so could save your family and your neighbors some serious aggravation, and yourself a nasty run-in with local law enforcement. Try to create a "V" shape with baffles in front of your speaker to capture the best tone.

31 AVOID AMP HEAD VIBRATION

If you're recording a guitar through a speaker cabinet with a separate head, keep the head off the speaker to avoid any unwanted rattle or sound degradation caused by head vibration. Also, if you're planning on enclosing the cabinet with baffles, remember that a hot amp head could be a fire hazard.

32 GREAT SOUNDING POUNDING

Great sounding drum tracks are essential to a great sounding recording. If you're using samples, loops, or some kind of drum machine, you've probably already got it mostly in the can. If you're recording live drums however, you can follow this simple mic configuration for capturing the best sounds and ensuring that your tracks have an awesome foundation.

Of course, you can use any microphone you have available. But the classic drum miking arrangement includes the following:

- A Shure SM-57 on the bass drum routed to track 1

- A Shure SM-57 on the snare drum routed to track 2

- One or more mics on the toms routed to tracks 3 and 4

- Two condenser mics overhead to capture the cymbals (as well as the room sound of the whole kit) routed to tracks 5 and 6

- If your music involves precision hi-hat work (and if your drummer is really crisp), you may want to add another mic solely for the hi-hat, routed to track 7

- You might also want to place an additional mic under the snare drum to more effectively capture the sound of the snare itself—especially if you're recording hard rock or heavy metal, for which you'll want more crack to the snare.

If you don't have that many tracks to allot to drums, you may be able to condense the toms and overheads through the use of subgroups on your mixer—just remember that when using subgroups, pan them opposite each other. Another option is to designate a separate, smaller mixer specifically for mixing several drum mics down to two stereo signals into your recording deck. If you choose to do this, make sure that you're happy with the mix, though, because once it's done, it's done—there's no changing it if the hi-hat is too loud, or the crash too quiet.

As for mic placement, you'll want to experiment a little; but the general rule of thumb is to mic your drums tight—place the mic as close to the heads as possible without touching or interfering with the drummer's ability to play. Some engineers like to mic the toms and snare a little looser, however, so that the tom mics pick up the cymbals and the snare mic picks up the hi-hat. When you mic the bass drum, insert the microphone into the drum and closer to the side of the shell, where you'll pick up more of the drum's overtones, rather than the middle of the drum.

Drum mic clips—even whole drum mic *kits*—can really take the guesswork out of the placement issue, and can be purchased pretty inexpensively these days.

TRACK 6

33 D.I. THAT GUITAR

Not thrilled with your electric guitar tone or the "house" amplifier? Other than recording your electric guitar off an amp through a microphone, consider splitting your signal and recording a D.I. (direct input) guitar to another available track. This way, if the original performance was good, but the recorded tone not so good, you can run the D.I. track back through a different amp or preamp and re-record it. You can even use the D.I. track—probably with some EQ and effects—together with your original amp track to fix the tonal deficiencies of the original. The truth is, if your only amp is the one that came with your Squier Strat Pack, you may find yourself doing this kind of thing quite often.

TRACK 7

34 MIKING PIANOS

If you're lucky enough to have a real, live piano (and piano player) at your disposal, take advantage of the situation and dedicate everything you've got to capture this incredible sound! If you mike your piano carefully, you'll add a resonance and reality to your recording that no synthesizer could ever match. Use your best condenser or ribbon mics to capture the full frequency range of the instrument. Before recording, check your mic placement and levels by playing all the notes chromatically up and down the keyboard. Also be mindful that hammers and pedals may be noisy.

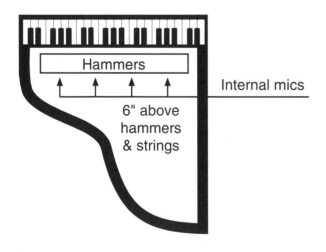

Grand Piano. To mike a grand piano, place one mic near the hammers, about six inches above where the hammers hit the strings, and toward the center of the keyboard. If you have enough mics and available tracks (hey, you can always ping-pong down—how often do you get to record a grand piano?), experiment with placing separate mics above the hammers and somewhat evenly spaced along the keyboard in order to separately capture the highs, mids, and lows. Keep your EQ settings flat until after recording, unless something really sounds amiss.

Regardless of your interior mic placement, be sure to place another mic outside the fully propped-open lid of the piano, the mic pointing toward the bottom of the lid. This placement will pick up the gloriously full sound being reflected off the bottom of the open lid. If you can, place other mics near where the strings are attached (at the center for the high- and middle-register strings; toward the far end of the piano for the lower-register strings). Don't bother with the room sound unless the room sounds fantastic—close miking a grand piano alone will give you outrageous sounds with which to work. Of course, if you've got the spare mics…go for it. You can never have enough sonic snapshots of a grand piano or other such rare studio instruments.

Upright Piano. To mike an upright piano, place one mic over the open top of the piano and another inside the piano. If possible, place a third mic outside the piano behind the soundboard (you'll want to move the piano slightly away from the wall, if possible, and preferably angled so as to create a mini isolation booth between the piano and the wall for this mic). Place your room mics about five feet off the ground and about four feet away from the piano.

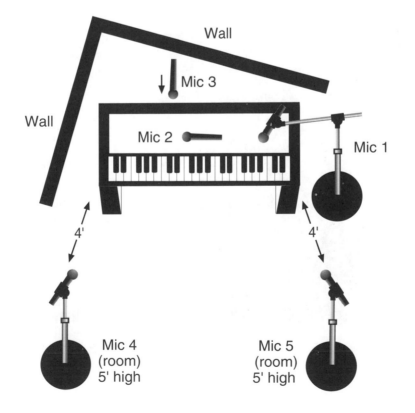

Brass and woodwind instruments—including saxophone, trumpet, trombone, flute, piccolo, oboe, clarinet, recorder, etc.—can be miked a in variety of different ways depending on your situation, as different instruments, different players, and different rooms will all present their own benefits or challenges. And yes, you can mike these instruments according to the following instructions, but as always, experimentation is key. Move your mics around and listen for the best sound. (For more information about general miking techniques and finding the best mic positioning, see tip #24.)

- While for live recording situations, you might be conditioned to place a microphone inside the bell of a horn, you don't necessarily have to do this for studio recording, unless you are experiencing bleed-through from other nearby instruments such as drums or guitars.

- Try miking a saxophone (or other type of horn) either near the bell, near the mouthpiece, or even near the middle of the instrument. The difference in tonal characteristics will be amazing. Try blending these sounds.

- With flute, piccolo, recorder, etc., place a microphone over the finger holes, approximately two feet either above the instrument or in front of it. Also, moving the mic closer to the embouchure will emphasize the breathiness of the tone.

- Try miking a clarinet or oboe at both the bell and above the keys.

- Try both close and distance miking. You may find, however, that placing your mic from one to three feet from the instrument will give you a more realistic sound overall, since no one (except maybe the instrument's player) usually hears the horn the way a close mic will hear it. Most of us will be not be positioned as close to the instrument as its player, and so will hear it from some degree of distance, and usually with some room ambience mixed in.

- Try distance room mics—especially in a room with strong reverberation characteristics—and blend them with your closer mics.

- When recording more than one brass or woodwind instrument at a time, miking each instrument separately allows for the most control during mixdown. However, you can strike a good balance by miking the instruments collectively with a pair of mics in a standard XY setup, with the mics placed as equidistantly between the instruments as possible, and approximately two to three feet away.

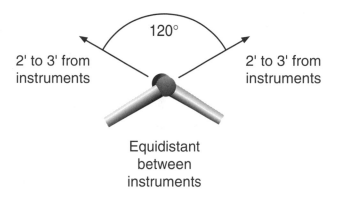

- Change the position of the musicians themselves if necessary to achieve a balanced sound when recording a group or section.

- Listen for excessive wind noise coming out of the bell of a horn. Also be aware of potentially noisy pads and other workings on brass or wind instruments. Change your microphone positions accordingly to reduce these sounds in your recorder, or use EQ to reduce their presence on your recording.

- Be aware of excessive "human" wind noises (and no, ha, ha, I'm not talking about the "pull-my-finger" type). Think of how noticeable Jethro Tull flautist Ian Anderson's breathing is on many of his recorded flute solos. You can move microphones to reduce this noise if you want, but you may choose to keep some of this sound in the mix to retain the character and trademark stylings of the player (especially if they're the hot local horn player whom you're paying to appear on your recording, or whom you're planning to "feature" in your liner notes or on your CD cover to help sell more copies).

- Brass instruments have a very full dynamic range: from very quiet to very loud. Be careful when using sensitive condenser or ribbon microphones on these instruments; it's better to position condenser and ribbon mikes farther away from these instruments, and to position only dynamic mics at close range.

- Condenser mics will more accurately capture the tonality and dynamics of woodwind instruments.

- Use dynamic mics to close mic whistles, which can easily distort or damage sensitive condenser mics. If you must use a condenser mic on a whistle, you'll probably have to roll of the high frequencies in your mix.

Violin, viola, cello, and double or upright bass have very distinct tonal characteristics and very large dynamic ranges. To capture these beautiful instruments accurately, try the following:

- Use condenser or ribbon mics for recording stringed instruments. Try a small-diaphragm mic for violin and viola, a large-diaphragm mic for cello and bass.

- When recording violin or viola, use a tall boom stand for placing a microphone from two to five feet above the instrument.

- To achieve a scratchier, more hoedown-like fiddle sound with more attack, place a microphone closer to the f-holes or bridge of the instrument. For a more mellow sound, aim the microphone toward the neck of the instrument.

- Position the musician in the corner of a room. Then place a tall boom stand with a microphone facing upward toward the corner's ceiling to capture the room sound reflected off the intersection of the walls and ceiling. Mix this signal with that of your closer mic—but be attentive to possible phase cancellation.

- For cello or bass: place a microphone over the bridge for a brighter sound; aim the microphone into the f-hole for a fuller sound. For a complete sonic snapshot, try one mic on the bridge or f-hole, and one mic on the neck.

 37 MIKING A ROTATING SPEAKER

If you have the great fortune of including the sounds of an actual Hammond B3 organ and/or a Leslie-style rotating speaker cabinet in your recordings, the following mic configurations will optimize their effects. Try placing one mic at the top louver only of the cabinet, or try aiming two mics at both the top and bottom louvers of the cabinet. Also, try placing a mic approximately six feet away from the cabinet at the height of the rotating speaker.

Another alternative would be these miking techniques that I learned from the Allman Brothers' late producer, Tom Dowd:

- Place one mic on the side of the cabinet and a second mic at the front or back of the cabinet, so the mics are 90 degrees to each other.

- Place both mics 90 degrees off-axis to the speaker(s). Dowd told me this off-axis miking technique could add as much as 6 db gain in recording level with minimum meter deflection (regardless of whether it is used with a Leslie cabinet, a bass drum, or acoustic instruments).

- Dowd insisted that the wrong way to mic a Leslie cabinet was with two mics placed on either side of the cabinet, both on-axis—doing so causes serious phase cancellation.

 38 MIKING VOCALISTS

Most vocalists will benefit from the application of a large-diaphragm condenser microphone, though you may want to use a small-diaphragm condenser on a female vocalist if you're looking for increased high end. However, if your singer insists on screaming into the mic, or if you want to capture an "earthier" vocal tone, you might opt for a dynamic mic instead. In general, the closer a vocalist stands to the mic, the more presence the vocals will have—but also more unwanted breathiness and potentially noticeable crackling sounds. Reduce these undesirable noises by having the singer stand back about six inches from the mic.

When miking multiple singers or a small chorus, first make sure the loudest and most powerful singer is in the middle of the ensemble and back a step or two, then place a single microphone six to eight feet from the entire group. If you're recording a larger chorus, break them into two or three smaller sets and close mic each set with separate microphones placed from one to three feet from the singers' mouths. (Also see tip #21 and tip #18.)

39 MIKING PERCUSSION

With the Allman Brothers, late producer Tom Dowd got plenty of experience recording Latin percussion instruments—particularly conga drums. A common configuration for recording congas is to place a mic above the heads of the drums in order to capture the slaps of the hands. But Dowd told me he preferred to also capture the congas' beautiful, deep, resonant low end, so he would place an omnidirectional mike in between the two drums, on the floor, facing up. Doing so captures both the slap and all the low end. You can actually get an enormous sound out of these drums; but typically, their sound on most recordings is very minimal and mid-rangy.

As for other small percussion instruments, such as tambourines, bells, maracas, etc., a small diaphragm condenser mic placed fairly close to the instrument is your best bet. Obviously, your options will change depending on whether you're recording a percussionist live with a band, or overdubbing instruments one at a time in a quiet studio. Do not subject an expensive condenser mic to extreme sound pressure levels by placing it inside or too near a drum—you'll likely ruin the microphone. But otherwise, condensers are perfect for picking up the high-frequency sounds that emanate from many of the hand-held percussion instruments.

TRACK 8

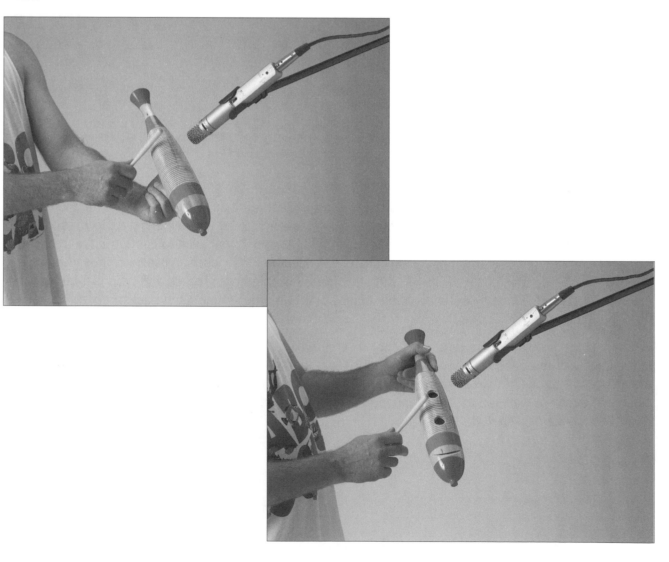

40 MONITOR-BUCKERS

Especially in this day and age of home computer recording, beware of noise from your computer screen coming through your guitar's single-coil pickups. If you're going to be doing a lot of recording in close proximity to your computer monitor, you might want to replace your single-coil pickups—or use a guitar with humbucking pickups. There are numerous guitar pickups on the market today: there are humbuckers that fit your guitar's single-coil slot (some of these pickups can fairly accurately mimic the tones of a single-coil pickup), as well as various other types of "noiseless" pickups. If you can't—or just don't want to—change the pickups on your guitar, at least reduce any potential noise from your monitor by turning it off while tracking, turning your back to it, and moving as far away from it as possible.

41 TUNE UP!

Tune all instruments before you record, and preferably with the same tuner. You'd be surprised at the number of pro recording sessions that became twice as costly just because by the artist(s) didn't tune up before starting (they were "going with the feeling" instead). The result is that, when overdubbing or fixing a mistake, either everyone has to tune to that (or those) out-of-tune instrument(s)—which is often not only time-consuming, but frustrating—or all kinds of electronic tomfoolery must be undertaken to bring the offending instrument(s) back in line with a true A 440 (or whichever intended pitch). And hey, even if you're not paying the big bucks for a pro studio, but are just laying down some rehearsal demos in your basement, you're still investing your time—and time is money, right? Besides, many an original demo makes it to a hit album because the vibe was just unmatchable. So, make sure you're in tune (and then the only headaches you'll have will be from your bandmates screaming, "I can't hear my part!").

42 MIDI INSTRUMENTS USE SUBS

If your recorder or mixer is short on input channels but has subgroups or submasters, you can use the subs as an input for your MIDI instruments—which saves your regular inputs for instruments that don't have their own internal EQ and effects, such as guitars, drums, or vocals. Because MIDI instruments have built-in EQ and effects, you can simply plug them into the return on the subs, expanding your channel-challenged board.

43 QUANTIZATION

My early experiences with *quantization*—a method of electronically reorganizing the beats on which an instrument plays (and fixing rhythmic mistakes)—came courtesy of a great Ensoniq keyboard/sequencer I picked up in the early '80s. As a guitarist who had until then only dabbled in keys, I was totally new to the world of synths and electronic music. Most of the time, I was using the keyboard to lay down drum and bass grooves for my original, guitar-based rock tunes, and I wasn't always very good at nailing the beat with the keys. The "quantize" function became a good friend at first, but I quickly tired of how mechanical it sounded. Thankfully, quantization technology and techniques have advanced tenfold since then.

Today, most sequencers allow much more accurate and realistic quantization than my old Ensoniq. Quantization—sometimes referred to as "auto-correct"—involves the process of electronically breaking down the beats, usually designated as "PPQ," or "pulses per quarter-note." In the early '80s, a typical sequencer, like that built into my Ensoniq keyboard, could only manage 24 to 96 PPQ. Today, sequencers routinely handle 960 PPQ, or more.

The major plus in these advances is that this increased definition allows you to make your tracks— particularly your drum tracks—sound much more realistic or "human," if you will, even if you're using a drum machine or hit-based samples to create your grooves. You can even quantize live drum recordings, provided you've separated the drums onto independent tracks. Really, you can quantize any instrument, on any track, if your software or hardware has quantization features. You can quantize an entire track at once, just a few bars, or even a single note/hit/event. And of course, you can choose not to quantize at all, if you prefer. In most applications, you can work with quantization while viewing your track as musical notation, piano roll, waveform, or whatever your preferred editing view.

Most quantize functions allow for you to change "value" and "percentage." Value choices usually include typical musical note designations, such as quarter, eighth, sixteenth, etc. Telling your sequencer to quantize your snare and bass tracks to eighth notes will snap any early or late hits right in line with the nearest eighth note, either forward or backward, depending on whether the drum hit before or after the beat. But do this knowing that tracks on which the hits all fall exactly on the beat do sound extremely mechanical, because no human being ever plays exactly on the beat throughout an entire song.

That's where percentage comes in. With percentage, you can tell your sequencer to move the snare hits—for example, 50 or 75 or 41 percent of the way toward the next nearest eighth note (or sixteenth, or thirty-second, etc.), or whatever sounds and feels right to you. Experimentation with your available quantizing parameters is key to learning how best to use quantization to your benefit, and to your liking.

Here are some helpful tips for using quantization:

- For natural sounding grooves, record without quantization; then quantize selectively later, if necessary.

- Explore quantization templates when available in your application. These may speed the process of creating the groove you're looking for.

- Some sequencers offer a factory-installed "human feel" quantization template that often is too random to truly feel human. Most humans don't play randomly, but consistently with their own quirks—always a little behind the beat, for instance, if you're talking about Rolling Stones drummer Charlie Watts. Go ahead and try the human feel option to see if you like it, but also try analyzing your own stylistic quirks, and then try to emphasize and assist them with more specific quantization moves—not wipe them out with the push of a button.

- Try quantizing manually by viewing a track in piano-roll and moving notes/hits/events that sound or feel too far from the beat. Then listen again, and don't be afraid to press "Undo" if you don't like your change.

- Save an unquantized version of the file or track as a backup, in case you make drastic quantization changes then decide you don't like them. Sometimes Undo can't Undo everything.

- Experiment with shortening some notes and lengthening others while you quantize them to create a smoother *legato* or more defined *staccato*. Let your ears be your guide.

- Use the "swing" option, if you have it (it may be located in your software menu under or near "percentage" options) to, well, *swing* the groove a little. This works especially well with dance, blues, and jazz recordings, as well as on instrumental solos.

- Try quantizing only the bass drum and/or snare at first, or only the hi-hat or ride cymbal.

- Try delaying your hi-hat or ride a bit, perhaps 1/96ths or 2/96th s of a quarter note. Try this with the snare too, or almost any rhythm section instrument. Do any global quantization to these tracks before you do this manual work.

- Move your crash cymbals slightly ahead of the beat—particularly leading into a big chorus or musical interlude—to add drama.

- Quantize instruments—such as the bass guitar or horns—more tightly to the beat when they're accompanying, and less tightly—if at all—when they step out into the spotlight. This is where your percentage parameter comes in handy.

- Analyze the final results of your quantizing to make sure you didn't move a note in the wrong direction. If so, fix that note manually.

44 MAKE IT SWING

Rhythm has really emerged in the past decade as a primary element in the success of today's hit songs—particularly hip-hop and dance tracks (but then, was good rhythm ever actually *unimportant?*). A lot of these songs' drum tracks "swing the sixteenths" (and believe me when I say that copping that swing feel is easier than copping a… uh, never mind).

To swing your sixteenths, lay down your basic groove with your drum kit, drum machine, or loops. Now delay the second and fourth 16th notes of each beat just a little, primarily on the hi-hat, but on any other rhythm instruments that hit on those beats as well. This is an excellent job for quantization, as described in tip #43, or for MIDI effects controllers, as discussed in tip #1 and tip #7.

45 A CURE FOR HICCUPS

If you're using Acid or a similar software program to put together your drum, percussion, or rhythm tracks, and you're experiencing hesitation or "hiccups" in the transitions between tracks (such as between your verse drum loop and your chorus drum loop), chances are you haven't drawn in the offending loop accurately enough. Instead, you may have dragged the loop into its assigned track, then stretched it, or altered it in some way that is preventing it from starting on its downbeat. If you're using professionally prepared loops and this happens, chances are that the loop is starting on the downbeat correctly, and it's you who has messed it up.

But this is an easy fix: first, erase or delete that loop (or section of that loop). Then drag its replacement back into place again from the original loop sample, and draw or place that replacement loop in its assigned track; this time being more careful to line up the downbeat and the subsequent beats against the time code ruler. Acid is pretty good at drawing in a loop to begin exactly on its downbeat.

TRACK 9

46 STACK YOUR TRACKS

Twenty-first-century rock producers are laying down some of the heaviest, densest-sounding rhythm tracks ever recorded. But that's easy to do when you're using software recording systems such as Pro Tools or Acid Pro and have an *unlimited* number of tracks at your disposal. In the old days, someone like Led Zeppelin's Jimmy Page—a pioneer of guitar overdubbing—might have put down as many as eight different guitar tracks to create his lush productions. Today, however, a producer may simply duplicate a guitar track several times to get the crunchy, bottom-heavy sound heard on many current rock hits.

If you're using Pro Tools, Acid Pro, or a similar program such as Cakewalk Sonar, simply lay down your initial tracks, then use the software's "duplicate track" function to add as many extra dupes of that track as you want. You'll hear the density increase with each additional track.

If you have a digital stand-alone-type recording deck, you can use the "copy" or "duplicate" functions to dupe tracks. However, if your stand-alone system is not digital, you may have to do this the old-fashioned way: by ping-ponging your initial track over to other available tracks. Either way, you're guaranteed to hear the crunch factor multiply.

You can use this process on the recording of any instrument, too—try it on your drum and bass tracks as well as your guitar. And why stop there? Go ahead and try this on vocals as well—especially the "shout" background styles. After you've mastered this, try fattening the sound even more by using the technique described in tip #85.

TRACK 10

"ENLARGE" THE ROOM

When you're confined to recording in a small home studio, you're simply not going to be able to accurately duplicate the big room sounds you've heard on many of your favorite recordings. In order to get the kind of sounds that recording in a big room can accomplish, major artists often rent out mansions, churches, and other halls with massive rooms, high ceilings, and plenty of hard, reflective surfaces—such as wooden floors or stone fireplaces—in which to record their albums.

One of the very best acoustic guitar sounds I ever captured was in the living room of a mansion in Northern California. The floors were wooden, the ceiling was more than two-stories high, and the stone fireplace was almost large enough to walk into—it filled nearly one whole wall. There was another wall that was almost entirely all windows. My acoustic guitar simply vibrated with ambient resonance when I strummed, and the whole, huge room seemed to amplify the sound. I'm still hoping to buy that house someday, just because of that sound (well, there was also this girl, but that's another issue).

Anyway, while you're probably not ready to tear down any walls or raise any ceilings in your own studio, you can make your room sound bigger—particularly with regard to your drum and guitar sounds—by simply adding delay to your room mics. Place your drums or amplifier on one end of the room, and your room mics on the other; then add between 5 and 30 milliseconds of delay to each of your room mics. Make sure to delay them more or less equally. These settings will approximate the increased travel time of sound waves in a much larger room, and will definitely increase the aurally apparent size of your studio.

TRACK 11

 # USE ONE EAR TO JUDGE

A microphone hears sounds the same way one of your ears hears sounds; not the way both of your ears hear collectively. Your ears and your brain work together to interpret sound—canceling out extraneous frequencies from sound waves that arrives at slightly different times and pitches in each ear as a result of the various reflective surfaces that the sound encounters on its way to each ear. Microphones—and particularly room microphones—can't filter or cancel out these muddying sound waves, and thus your recording may suffer due to bad mic placement.

To judge the true sound of a room, and to find the best location for your room microphones when distance-miking a drum set, guitar amp, acoustic piano, or any other acoustic instrument (including the human voice), analyze the sound in the room using only one ear. Stick a finger in one ear or seal it off completely with your hand while you move around the room, listening intently for the room's "sweet spot" for a particular instrument.

The sweet spot should be a place where the sound is richest and most expansive, yet not boomy or lacking in frequency depth. You may find that the sweet spot of the room is close to, or away from, a particular wall, depending on the room's size, shape, and objects (furniture, curtains, wall-hangings, etc.), and the placement of your instrument. If there isn't a clear winner in terms of the sweet spot's location, you may want to move your instrument a bit and search again. Once you find the spot(s) that work best, you'll probably always want to arrange your instruments and mics in a similar fashion within that same room. Remember, every room will be at least somewhat, if not drastically, different from others. (For more on room mic placement, see tip #20 and tip #47).

49 TUNING DRUMS

Out-of-tune drums add all kinds of horrible harmonics to the low-end and midrange of your mix, muddying up the sound in a way most people can't put into words (other than such pithy epithets as "sucks," and "#&%$!"). Mostly though, they just know it sounds sort of warbled. Tuning drums is actually relatively easy. Hit the drum a short distance from the rim next to each lug nut on the top (and, if they're on, bottom) drumheads. Each drum should be in tune to a single pitch all the way around the rim. What pitch(es) should you tune to? That's up to you. There are many schools of though on this issue. Some drum manufacturers, such as DW, actually stamp a note name on each drum shell, indicating the note they deem that shell most resonant with.

Typically, the bottom head of a drum is tuned to the fundamental of the drum shell, if that pitch can be determined. The top head is normally tuned lower (slightly less tension) than the bottom head, often a fifth down—though some drummers tune each head equally, or even tune the top head higher than the bottom head.

Also, check the tuning of the bass drum against the bass guitar. Sometimes their combination will cause a warbling as well as overtones that create a generally out-of-tune sound (for which most people blame the bass player). Have the bassist check his or her tuning; then turn your attention to the bass drum, and either tighten or loosen the bass drum heads until the problem is resolved. This operation may require a fine degree of listening, but it will get easier after you've done it a few times.

As for muffling out unwanted rings or noises, use the subtlest touch you can. Check for and tighten loose hardware, applying minute amounts of duct tape if necessary. You can also make small tubes of duct tape and place them directly on the drumheads for a slight muffling effect. The more tape you use, the greater the muffling. The drum products known as O-rings will also create a pronounced muffling effect. If you put a pillow or blanket inside the bass drum, don't allow it too much contact with the heads—you want it to dampen the sound, not choke it off completely.

In addition, know that many engineers prefer to work with small drums, saying they sound bigger on tape—much the way a small guitar amplifier is often preferred over a larger amp. Smaller drums can be tuned lower while still maintaining tension on the heads. Also, thinner, lighter shells resonate better than heavy shells. And thinner heads have higher fundamentals and longer sustain than thicker, coated, or multi-ply heads. Of course you may or may not have control over the type of drums or drumheads, unless you're planning to purchase your own drum set for your studio—in which case, you can set it up for optimal tone right from the start.

 50 PUMP UP THE DRUMS

Unless you record solo acoustic instruments with no percussion, drum tracks are what typically drive your recordings. And how well your drum tracks serve this purpose often depends on how good you are at incorporating compressors, limiters, gates, and reverb into your recording.

Even if you don't have a high-priced compressor—or any of those other fun gadgets most pro studios swear by—you can still boost the impact of your drum and percussion tracks (and any track, really) with a simple guitar stomp-box compressor.

By running either a feed of your complete drum mix (ping-ponged down to one track), or just your kick or snare, out of your recorder, through the stomp-box, and then back into your recorder (but on a track different from your original percussion tracks). Monitor the returning signal solo, compress the hell out of it, then blend it together with the original in your mixer (with the compressed track level set to taste); you'll just have added impact to your original drum mix.

TRACK 12

51 BAFFLE YOUR BASS DRUM

In addition to putting a microphone inside your bass drum, there's another technique that will give you a really intense kind of bass drum sound that you might want on a dance track or a seriously pumping rock chorus. Because lower frequencies create big, long sound waves, when given a little room, they'll develop better further from the drum.

So try this technique to get a seriously boomy bottom on your recordings: baffle the front of your bass drum by arranging some chairs, guitar amps, sawhorses (hey, how about real baffles?), or whatever as a scaffolding over which you can drape a blanket to create a four-foot-or-so-long tunnel in front of the front drum head. Then stick a mic inside this tunnel, at the far end, away from the drum (you don't need to close off the far end of the tunnel, though that might help).

TRACK 13

Bass drum

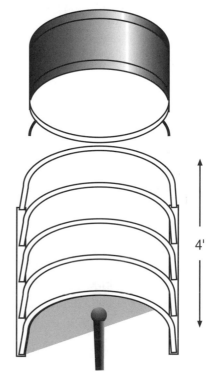

4'

NON-DESTRUCTIVE EDITING

Most people take their new recorder (or recording software) out of the box and just start laying down tracks just as quickly as they can, without taking the time to really learn all the features their new toy has to offer. One of the coolest functions on modern hard disk recorders—one that pro engineers and producers use on their systems with regularity—is basically your good old computer cut-and-paste operation. Of course, in the world of recording, this action is more often referred to by the kinder, gentler euphemism, "non-destructive editing."

With non-destructive editing you can move or remove, copy, or paste entire sections of your song—or perhaps, more importantly, sections of individual tracks—with just a few clicks of a key (or mouse). By way of your hard disk-based system's editing features, you can completely rearrange your songs; then, if you don't like a new version, simply undo until you're back to the original.

For instance, my Akai DPS16 allows a whole bunch of such editing options, including copy-overwrite, copy-insert, cut-overwrite, cut-insert, insert silence, cut-discard, cut-move, time stretch, and stretch-move. Unfortunately, so many options mean that I could potentially mess up a really good thing; but fortunately, I've also got 250 levels of undo (ain't technology wonderful?)!

Let's say your bassist has a tendency to play rock-solid through the first verse and chorus of every song, but then suddenly decides he's Jaco Pastorius and goes off on a jazz-fusion binge that totally distracts from *your* brilliant lead guitar work. Not to worry: after he's brushed the empty cans of barley soda off the studio couch and joined the snorus chorus, you can simply mark his first verse and chorus sections, copy them, then overwrite them throughout the rest of the song (eliminating all his absurdly placed sixteenth-note triplets and altered dominant arpeggios).

I once watched digital editor/assistant engineer Kevin Dickey do exactly this on the live Yes album, *Keys to Ascension* (I'm not sure if bassist Chris Squire knows about this though, so please don't tell him). I've also seen Steve Vai do this to tracks off his *Alive in an Ultra World* album as well. Nobody plays perfectly; and everybody copies their short sections of near-perfection and pastes them over their blunders. You can, too.

Learn to use these incredible features by editing like crazy on some throwaway track (i.e., like a bad rehearsal recording, or even a *copy* of a keeper session). Practice makes perfect, as they say; and after all, this is the way modern hit records are made.

 # RIDE THE FADERS

In the great Simon & Garfunkel hit, "The Boxer," the sound of the pedal-steel guitar was actually achieved not with a pedal steel (or even a guitarist faking a pedal steel), but by Paul Simon riding the faders on the mixing board while a trumpeter played the solo. Simon's trick can be applied to almost any instrument: swell the volume after the note has been sounded, and pull it back down before the note decays and the next note is played. You'll get a very steely sound out of any melodic instrument.

TRACK 14

 RECORD AS A GROUP

Legendary late producer Tom Dowd once told me that he preferred recording bands live in the studio (which he actually did on most of the Allman Brothers albums he produced) because—due partially to the leakage between microphones—the harmonic sum of the whole group playing together was greater than the sum of the individual parts had they been overdubbed. B.B. King also told me that he much prefers recording with a live band so as to get the feel of the other players through the camaraderie of hanging out together before and during the session—a camaraderie that creates a palpable emotional impact on the recording itself. If you can, record your band live, then overdub as necessary. It may take some practice to learn the best way to capture a live sound; but once you do, the end result will be much more lively—both from a performance and a technical/aural standpoint.

 LOCATION, LOCATION, LOCATION

In recording, as in real estate, location can be everything. This is particularly true for hard disk recording, since a hard disk-based system probably allows you more tracks than you'll ever be able to fill up with ego-inflating guitar solos or wacky percussion sounds. Of course, such a virtual bonanza means that you'll be spending a lot of time overdubbing; so you'll want to know how to quickly maneuver through your basic tracks (from verse to chorus to solo, etc.), without having to listen to the whole song each time to get there.

With most systems these days it's pretty easy to set "locate points" at the beginnings of each section of your song before you start laying down overdubs or additional tracks. Right after you get the most basic of your basic tracks recorded—as in right after the drum/percussion track, if it's clear from that performance alone where the verse ends and the chorus begins—take the time to set your locate points. Your system probably allows you to set several locate points, and most likely, even allows you to name them (i.e., intro, break, verse 1, verse 2, chorus 1, bridge, chorus 2, solo, chorus 3, outro, etc.).

Getting yourself in the habit of setting up in this manner at the very beginning of each project, and you will drastically reduce the wasted, enthusiasm-draining time you'd otherwise spend between overdubs searching for song sections that require work. With your locate points set, you can lay down track after track on one instrument, in a variety of sections of your song, with virtually no waiting between takes; in addition, you'll probably even be able to loop your toughest section in order to rehearse it a few times before you hit "record." (Just try to get your band to do that for you).

 CLEAN AND DISTORTED

If your clean guitar track is overpowering your distorted guitar track, and you don't have any more head-room to bring the dirty guitar up—or if the two sounds are sharing a track—re-record your clean or acoustic guitar track 5 dB lower than you recorded the distorted guitar track to even them out. Remember that clean instruments always cut through the mix better than distorted instruments.

TRACK 15

57 GET SOME TRIM

If you find that you're regularly having to push a track fader above 0 dB, either your trim is too low or you've got an extreme EQ cut—which may not be intentional. First take a look at your trim pot to make sure it's set at an optimal level. Have the musician play the instrument exactly as they will during the recording, while you use your meters to assess and make trim adjustments as necessary. If trim is not the culprit, double-check your EQ settings to make sure that you haven't inadvertently nudged one of the controls into the "let's make Johnny's guitar sound like crap" realm.

58 MIXDOWN TIPS, PART 1:
PLACEMENT

One of the most important elements to a good final mix is to ensure that the placement of the instruments and effects make aural sense in a three-dimensional way. As you "look" at the band, is the bass player to your right or your left? Is the lead guitarist standing front-and-center when he or she solos, or is he or she hiding behind the keyboardist along the side of the stage? Is your lead vocalist standing in front of or behind your drummer?

Creating an accurate—or at least believable—audio image or "soundstage" of the band when playing in front of you should be as much of a goal as ensuring that all the instruments and voices are heard clearly. You'll want to attempt to give each player a little elbow-room, so to speak, by carving out a space for him or her. Here are some tips to help you achieve that goal:

- **Front-to-back placement and instruments**. Think of your stage in terms of front-to-back depth, place your instruments accordingly, and use volume, reverb, and delay, as appropriate for each instrument. Certainly the Rolling Stones' stage is deeper than your local jam-night stage—from where Mick Jagger stands to where Charlie Watts sits. Decide how deep your stage is and position instruments accordingly.

- **Front-to-back placement and volume**. Front-and-back placement is controlled primarily by volume. Louder sounds closer; quieter sounds farther. Make your lead instruments or lead vocals louder than anything else in your mix; that way, they'll sound as though they're out in front of the band as you "watch" them from your front-and-center seats in your imaginary concert hall. Accompanying instruments should be quieter.

- **Front-to-back placement and reverb**. Front-and-back placement can also be controlled by reverb. The more reverb, the farther away the sound seems. Adjust the reverb for each instrument so as to position them closer or farther back in the mix.

- **Front-to-back placement and delay**. Front-and-back placement can also be controlled by delay. Sound travels at a certain speed; adding a 5 ms delay to a signal will make it sound approximately 5 feet farther away than an equally panned signal with no delay.

- **Front-to-back placement and panning and delay together.** Use panning *and* delay to move the placement of your instruments from left to right on the stage and position them as they might be on a real stage. Think of the stage as a clock: center stage at straight-up 12 midnight, far stage right at 9 PM, and far stage left at 3 PM. But, you say, your pan knobs go beyond that, to like 7 PM. and 5 PM. Consider those extreme hard-left and hard-right positions to be the reflective walls of the concert hall, beside and even behind some of the audience, and reserve them for delays, echos, and reverbs, just like in a real concert hall.

- **Left-and-right placement and panning**. Left-and-right placement is controlled primarily by panning. That's easy to envision if you have only one track of a certain instrument (turning the pan knob on that track left sends the instrument to the left, etc.). But you can achieve finer degrees of left/right placement control when you have identical or near identical signals on two tracks, panned differently. And for higher-quality mixes, you're likely to have doubled up many of your tracks anyway, particularly your lead vocal or lead guitar tracks.

- **Left-and-right placement and delay**. Left-and-right placement can also be controlled by delay. For example, if you have a stereo sound source panned equally left and right, and with no delay on either side, the sound will actually seem to be coming from the center. Now add a delay of up to 28 ms to the right side of that sound, and the source of the sound will seem to move to the *left* on our stage—and even farther left as you approach 28 ms. By the time you get up to 35 ms of delay, however, the signal will change from a directional cue to a distinct and separate echo of the original sound. Obviously, panning alone can also be used to achieve this illusion; but since you probably won't be working with many completely dry signals when doing your final mixes, use the delay to your advantage as a placement tool.

Another very important element to the process of "carving out a space" involves the use of EQ layering, discussed in further detail in tip #60.

TRACK 16

59 MIXDOWN TIPS, PART 2:
ODDS AND ENDS

When it comes time to do your final mixes, you're going to want fresh ears and a relaxed and enthusiastic attitude. Don't plan on doing final mixes immediately after a couple of hours of final tracking, track clean up, or other prep work. Get all that stuff out of the way and start on your final mixes on a new day. Here are some other helpful suggestions:

- **Channel labeling**. Use either drafting or masking tape to label your mixer channels; that way, you won't waste time and energy trying to remember which instrument is on which track move the wrong fader, or run the risk of ruining a track altogether.

- **Faders**. Set your master fader to 0 dB or slightly hotter before you start mixing. At the end of your mix, if you're pegging all your meters and distorting your monitor speakers, you can pull the master down a little and still maintain your mix—instead of pulling all the faders down individually and messing up your mix.

- **Compression**. Add a little compression to the lead vocals during your final mix. Even if you used a compressor when you recorded them, this final bit of compression may be the trick that makes your singer cut through and really catch peoples' ears. Try compressing these tracks at a medium ratio (4:1 or so) and a medium threshold; also use soft-knee compression.

- **Reverb**. Try a bit of reverb and a 100 to 250 ms slapback delay on the lead vocals to fatten them up a bit.

- **Panning**. Instruments that fall in the same general frequency range as the lead vocals—such as guitars and keyboards—should be panned away from the voice. Also, consider using more than one lead vocal track panned slightly away from one other to give the vocalist a bigger sound.

- **EQ**. Consider cutting EQ on any instruments in the 1 kHz range.

- **Mark your mixes**. Make and save multiple mixes, noting the changes between them. Then, on another day, when your ears are fresh again, audition all your mixes and choose either the best mix and make it your final, or the best and make it better.

- **Save your mixes**. Make and mark duplicate copies of your final mixes, and save them in different locations (not on the same computer, for example), to protect your work should disaster strike.

60 LAYERS, LAYERS, LAYERS

Listen to Eric Clapton's rhythm guitar tone on "After Midnight" to hear how producer Delaney Bramlett layered this track in between the important keyboard and bass instruments. Clapton's rhythm guitar is thin and crunchy to make room for the keys, bass, and hi-hat; all which help drive the song. By itself, Clapton probably would have hated that tone; but heard the way Bramlett situated it, it is perfectly placed to get attention, yet allow the other instruments room to breathe. Jimmy Page did a similar thing with his guitar tone on the Led Zeppelin classic "Rock 'n' Roll": he dialed in a very mid-rangy EQ on the rhythm guitar (probably using a wah pedal), which added definition, yet allowed John Paul Jones's bass guitar and piano to be heard clearly.

The technique that these producers used EQ to give each instrument its own untrampled space in the mix is called "layering," which really is an essential skill—your recordings will be vastly improved once you master it. I'll make this evident through the following hypothetical situation:

For the sake of simplicity, let's say you've recorded a band that includes lead and rhythm guitar, bass, drums, keys, and lead and background vocals. That's simple, right? And let's assume your musicians have their sounds so perfectly dialed in and that you had your microphones so perfectly placed that you could leave the EQ settings on the board perfectly flat on each and every track. You didn't boost or cut EQ in any range for any of the instruments or voices.

Now, as you attempt to do your final mix, you realize that the rhythm guitar isn't really cutting through—it sounds a little muddy and tangled up with the bass guitar, especially during the chorus where unison riffs are played. And your important keyboard riff in the bridge is sort of masked by the background vocals. Also, the outro guitar solo is causing your lead vocals to sound kind of de-emphasized—just when they need to be in everyone's face.

First, you might try cutting the guitar below 100 Hz and the bass between 200 and 300 Hz. This will add definition to both instruments. Then you might boost the guitar slightly in the 2.5 to 4 kHz range to bring out the attack. During the chorus, when the two instruments play in unison, you might even increase the amount of cut or boost temporarily to give each instrument a little more separation and clarity during that part of the song. Then, during the verses, you can back off on the cutting and boosting a little.

Next, to bring out and improve the of the keyboard in the bridge, you might cut the background vocals that fall below 250 Hz and in the midrange by between 2 and 4 kHz, and then bring the keys up in the 2–4 kHz range. If doing this seems to make the background disappear, you might boost them around 10 kHz to give them back a little of their sparkle.

And finally, on your outro, where the lead guitar was interfering with the big lead vocal finale: boost the vocals a few dB between 150 and 200 Hz, and again around 3 kHz and 10 kHz. Then, if it's necessary to return a little of the guitar's bite, cut the guitar a bit in these same frequency ranges, and boosting it around 5 kHz.

A really key element to layering is cutting one instrument in the same range that you boost another. Wherever two or more instruments are getting in each other's way, you'll want to cut the EQ of the less crucial instrument and boost the EQ of the more crucial one. Remember that the necessary prominence of each instrument will probably change throughout your song, as certain riffs, solos, or sweeteners take their turn in the spotlight. Also understand that your use of the stereo field—which you'll access primarily through panning—will also come into play, as will your use of reverb and delay to affect the front-to-back placement of the sounds in your mix.

You might also find it useful to invest in an audio frequency analyzer to truly dial in the layering of your mix. A frequency analyzer lets you to see a visual representation of the EQ settings for each of your soloed tracks, giving you a more empirical basis on which to make EQ cutting and boosting decisions. Basic frequency analyzers are available as free downloads off the Internet.

TRACK 17

61 FINDING THE FREQUENCY

I recently worked with Grammy-winning producer Jay Graydon on a whole series of recording articles, and for which Jay delved deeply into EQ techniques. Here is the method Jay recommends for finding the inherently good and bad frequencies in any instrument or voice, with which you can then make educated decisions regarding cutting or boosting the EQ in any range:

Jay suggests keeping your monitor level low and the EQ set flat and at zero gain. Solo the instrument or track you want to analyze, then bring the EQ gain (volume) up all the way on one band of your EQ (start with the midrange; do the highs and lows later). Now sweep through your EQ's entire frequency range of the mids by twisting the frequency pot through its full spectrum. For each particular instrument, you should hear areas within this entire range that sound good, and areas that sound bad—and every instrument will be different. After you've found the good frequencies, return the gain to zero, then add gain on that particular frequency or range to your taste.

If you're searching for bad-sounding frequencies to cut, start with the gain turned all the way down, and sweep the frequencies as described above. When you determine which frequencies you'd like to cut, return the gain to zero, then cut the desired frequency to suit your needs. After finding the frequencies you want to cut or boost, you should do so while listening to the full mix; not with the track soloed.

Also, be aware that loud, low frequencies can easily blow your monitor speakers or headphones. Do not use this sweeping technique on extremely low frequencies for low-end instruments, such as bass or kick drum. At the very least, simply reduce the amount of boost you use when attempting this sweep; perhaps limited to no more than 6 dB.

62 CUT BEFORE YOU BOOST

It's natural to want to boost the volume on anything you can't hear; but when you're recording music, cutting volume may actually be a better friend than boosting volume. In particular, cutting the volume of one EQ frequency in order to get it out of the way of another that you'd prefer to hear is key to quality recordings.

This technique is called "subtractive EQing." For instance, to make a lead vocal track less muddy, subtractive EQing may call for you to cut a few dB between 200 and 250 kHz rather than just immediately boosting the higher frequencies in an attempt to improve clarity. Other applications of subtractive EQing would be to cut the kick drum between 100 and 200 Hz so that the bass guitar will stand out more in that range—and therefore blend in better with the kick; and to cut a crunchy, distorted guitar track above 8 kHz to reduce amp noise and beef up the bottom end—instead of turning down your amp's gain (to reduce the noise) and boosting the EQ in the low end.

Pro engineers and producers have long been conditioned to cut before they boost because, in the days of analog recording, boosting always added noise. With most digital equipment, this problem has largely been eliminated; but it remains the tried-and-true method of dialing in a pro sound.

63 LESS EQ, MORE MIC TECHNIQUE

Adjusting the EQ always means the possibility of increased noise on your tracks. It's much better to become more adept at mic placement than to rely too heavily on EQ. By practicing good mic technique—whether you're a vocalist or an engineer deciding where to place a microphone to best capture a sound source—you'll need fewer EQ fixes, and will thus have less EQ-related noise in your recordings.

And in addition to simple distance issues related to microphone placement, you should work on finding and using your microphones' "sweet spots." Learn to hear the sweet spots vs. the "ugly spots," and you'll find yourself "fixing it in the mix" less often. (For more on microphone sweet spots, see tip #24.)

64 SEPARATE EQ SETTINGS

When you set a track's or an instrument's EQ, you'll often be tempted to leave it at that setting throughout the entire song. After all, you've found the settings you prefer for your guitar, vocals, and drums. Why mess with perfection, right?

Unfortunately, that level of sameness might give you an excellent recorded *sound*, but may be at least partially to blame for causing a monotonously ho-hum *song*. Sometimes you might want a punchier rhythm guitar during a chorus, a more laid-back acoustic during a verse, or a brighter hi-hat during a piano solo. Setting up different EQ parameters on individual tracks or sound sources can help you achieve this; but doing it on the fly is a recipe for disaster. Luckily, creating parallel tracks with different settings is not nearly as difficult as it sounds.

Simply route your signal to a new, clean track—either during or after recording the track (use a Y cable, separate microphones, or your recorder's internal routing capabilities to do this while recording the original track). On playback, mute the parallel track, and set your original track's EQ to your likings. Then mute the original track and make your desired changes to the parallel track's EQ. Obviously, you'll want to be listening to the appropriate part of the song (chorus, bridge, etc.) when making the EQ changes on the parallel track, to ensure that your EQ changes don't negatively affect the layering you've done on that section. Then, when you're doing your mix, you can use your mute buttons to simply alternate the tracks between on and off. Now punch up those choruses!

65 WOW! ARE THOSE REAL?

Audio enhancers and exciters—such as the BBE Sonic Maximizer or Aphex Aural Exciter—have been mainstays of professional studios for decades. Both of these devices have achieved near mythical status for their ability to make just about everything sound, well, better. Both hardware and software versions are available today, and the software is compatible with most computer-based recording systems, such as Cakewalk or Pro Tools. You can use these devices on individual tracks or instruments, or on your entire mix. Many pro engineers swear by them, and use them on everything—including mastering (though that's probably approaching overkill).

Some of the specific pluses attributed to enhancers and exciters are that they will improve vocal intelligibility, allowing listeners to understand a song's lyrics better without increasing the level of the lead vocal. Also, according to both the manufacturers and many of their most ardent fans, these items will help "bring the guitars out of the mud"; "add realism to the keyboards, synthesizers, and samples"; "expand the spatial dimension of stereo reverb and chorus"; make the "highs clearer, more naturally brilliant, and more finely detailed"; and make the "lows tighter, more well-defined, and harmonically richer." How could you go wrong with that?

Basically, these are just EQ tricks—although that assessment's a little simplistic. While the actual actions of these toys are somewhat shrouded in mystery, there is also some degree of phase cancellation and addition processing at work, as well as some amount of delay—particularly the allowing of the higher frequencies to arrive at your ear sooner than the lows, which increases the apparent clarity of the overall mix.

More realistically (at least in the case of the Sonic Maximizer), here's what's going on behind the scenes:

1. Bass frequencies below 100 Hz are boosted

2. High frequencies above 2 kHz are dynamically boosted based on midrange level

3. Either the mids or highs are flipped in phase.

With a little practice, most of this can be achieved on your board. Still, neither device is outrageously expensive, and they both work. Just go get them and try them yourself; if you don't like 'em, surely your friendly retailer will let you trade them back in for a refund or store credit.

66 COMPRESSOR/LIMITER BASICS

Right after you've picked out a recording deck, software package, monitor speakers, good headphones, microphones, and if necessary, a CD Burner, your next concern will probably be a compressor and/or limiter. They're practically mandatory in a recording studio; pro engineers use them on pretty much every track. Compressors are largely responsible for the overall sonic differences you may hear on your own recordings vs. what you hear on a pro CD or on the radio. In fact, radio stations take already compressed music and compress it even more for broadcast.

Basically, compression punches the music up a notch, giving it added presence and impact. Consequently, you do need to understand compressor basics, as well as those of their nearest cousins, limiters (and the two are often combined in one package, known as compressor/limiters), in order to really lift your recordings to a higher level of professionalism.

Both compression and limiting are all about dynamics and dynamic range, which is the separation between the loudest and softest levels on a recording. I run into extremes of dynamic range all the time on classical music CDs. Typically, I'm listening to them fairly quietly, like in putting-the-kids-to-bed situations. Unfortunately, many classical CDs seem to have been mastered without compression, because many times the orchestra or instrumentalists are playing so quietly I can barely hear them, which temps me to turn the volume of my CD player way up. Of course, if I do turn it up, within seconds the entire orchestra will come bashing in so loudly that it would not only wake my own kids, but those in my neighbors' houses as well. So I suffer through not hearing the quiet parts, just so the loud parts won't be *too* loud. (Don't they know about compressors at the plant that burns classical CDs? I think they need to visit the guy who masters AC/DC albums.)

Dynamic range also comes into play when discussing the specs of various pieces of electronic gear— your effects units, speakers, microphones, etc. Give them too much signal and they'll distort; not enough signal and noise will override the purity of the sound you're attempting to record. You've seen this parameter referred to as "signal-to-noise ratio."

Dealing with these issues is where compressors and limiters come into play. Let's say you're recording an acoustic guitar. Chances are the guitar will be played more aggressively during the choruses of the song than during the verses. You could probably make up for the subsequent rising and lowering of level by raising and lowering the faders or the trim knob on your deck during recording or mix-down—a process called "gain riding" or "riding the faders." But that's a rather imprecise method, and you may be busy elsewhere at the time—like maybe playing the above-mentioned guitar part. Besides, some sound sources are somewhat unpredictable, and may make accurate gain riding all but impossible, even for the best engineer.

Compressors and limiters were designed to ride the gain automatically and much more quickly and precisely than could ever be done by a human being. In a nutshell, compressors make the quiet parts a little louder, and the loud parts a little quieter. By comparison, limiters basically just put a top limit on the gain, eliminating any signal that goes over a pre-set level; in other words, limiters usually don't affect the quieter parts of the signal at all.

Compressors are fairly easy to understand. For each dB going into the compressor, only a fraction of that dB is put out. You, the engineer, control what that fraction will be, based on your need and preference. You also have control over the compressor's other parameters, including ratio, threshold, attack, and release (or decay). Some compressors also allow you to choose between "soft-knee" and "hard-knee" (normal) compression.

Here are the basic elements of compression and the workings of most compressors:

- **Ratio or compression ratio**. This is often noted as something along the lines of "3:1," "5:1," or "10:1." What those ratios represent is, for each 3, 5, or 10 decibels that go in, only 1 will come out. Clearly, a compression ratio of 3:1 will not affect your sound as much as a ratio of 10:1. Understand then that beyond gain riding, higher compression ratios can drastically modify your sound. Don't be afraid to explore the possibilities.

- **Threshold**. The threshold setting allows you to choose at what level the compressor kicks in. If you set the threshold low, even the lowest signal levels will cause the compressor to do its thing. If you set the threshold high, the compressor will work only on louder sounds. If you set the threshold too high, however, and nothing crosses the line, the compressor will never kick in. How you set the threshold is important because only the part of the signal that crosses the threshold will be compressed—not the entire signal.

- **Attack and release**. These settings allow you to choose both how quickly the compressor acts once a level crosses your chosen threshold, and how long the compressor will act upon the signal. Once released, the compressor will not act again until the threshold has once again been exceeded. Regardless of the attack and release settings, once the compressor kicks in, it kicks in with full compression, according to your chosen ratio settings.

- **Gain**. Some compressors have a "gain" knob. This feature allows you to use the compressor to color the sound—and eliminate peaks and too-quiet sections—and then turn the level back up to where it was when it went into the compressor.

- **Hard-knee and soft-knee**. The terms "hard-knee" (or normal) and "soft-knee" compression refer to settings featured on many compressors. A hard-knee or normal compression setting allows you to choose whether or not a signal is subjected to immediate, full compression after the threshold has been crossed; a soft-knee compression setting allows for a gradual transition—from no compression, through partial compression, to full compression—after the threshold has been crossed. Soft-knee compression is less obvious to the average listener and is very useful with lead vocals, on which you might want less apparent studio trickery attached to your typically masterful performance.

There are three types of compressors on the market these days, VCA (voltage controlled amplifier), photo-optical, and variable mu (or variable gain). Talk to your local recording pro or least-pushy retailer to understand the pros and cons of each. Price may determine your purchasing decisions here. If you're capable of building your own electronic devices, search the Internet for plans and schematics; then do it yourself and save a bundle on re-creations of the most revered (and expensive) compressors.

TRACK 18

67 COMPRESSOR TIPS

Compressors, like most musical devices, are not inherently complicated; but what you can do with them is boundless. Plan on a lot of experimentation with your compressor (as you should everything else in your studio, too). Also, understand that one compressor may be perfectly suited to some jobs while another compressor may serve you better on others. Experiment with these settings in the appropriate situations:

- **To compress or not compress**. You don't have to have the compressor on all the time or use it on every track. Compare the compressed and non-compressed signals and—based on the sound, not your desire to play with that expensive box—then decide.

- **Use your meters**. And an A/B auditioning process to help you decide how much compression is too much. You may not hear much apparent compression while you're turning the knobs, but your meters won't lie (depending, of course, on how well you've treated them). Even if you don't think you really hear much compression, be aware that a change in gain of a mere 6db is a serious change.

- **Sound level drops as threshold is lowered**. Level also drops as compression ratio is increased. If you like what the compressed signal sounds like, but need more level, you may need to compensate elsewhere in your signal chain.

- **Over-compressing**. Don't over-compress during tracking; you can always add more compression during mixdown, but you can't reduce compression once it's in there.

- **Vocals**. Use soft knee, low ratio, high threshold for experienced vocalists with good mic technique—they often control their own level by moving closer to and farther from the mic while singing. Also, too much compression on vocals may increase room and electronic noise and accentuate loud breathing. Be careful not to overdo it.

- **Bass.** Plan on using a compressor on the bass, as most bassists don't play with even dynamics. The compression will add sustain too—always a benefit to the player. Use soft-knee compression on softer tunes, and normal compression on harder-hitting tunes.

- **Extreme level peaks**. Chain two compressors together and set the first one up to act more as a limiter (with a high threshold and ratio) to cut any extreme peaks in level. The second compressor will then serve as your true compressor, smoothing out the signal.

- **Sibilance**. Some compressors have "side-chain" jacks, which allow for such things as inserting a high-pass filter in order to limit compression only to the high frequencies. This would serve to replace the device known as a "de-esser," which is used to reduce sibilance (often noted as the overabundance of the "s" sound on some vocal tracks).

 68 ADDING A HUMAN ELEMENT

Contrary to the advice of many top producers and engineers and that which I've described elsewhere in this book, you might actually want to try using *less* compression and limiting on your tracks—particularly your vocal tracks—instead of more. Again, I'll defer to the late Tom Dowd, who engineered and produced dozens of major label albums throughout a long career, beginning with his first recordings of Atlantic jazz roster artists in 1947, until his death in 2002.

Dowd advised me to record *without* the compressor/limiter whenever possible, especially on vocals. Instead, when you come out of the mic or mic preamp, go to a fader on your recorder. Then, raise the fader as necessary to support the low notes, and lower the fader as necessary to hold back the high notes (you won't be able to perform this task as fast as a limiter can, but doing so will add a human element to your track). Finally, rather than compressing everything, feed this human-element-enriched track to the limiter to achieve greater depth.

You may have to make a couple of runs at the track to learn exactly where you might have to raise or lower the faders; and you can always use the compressor/limiter as a backup if necessary (as Dowd admitted he did). But still, the more you perfect your technique before sending the signal through the electronics, the better your recordings should sound, right? If it worked for Tom when he was producing Aretha Franklin and Ray Charles, it will probably work for you, too.

 69 COOL, LOW-FI, AM RADIO EFFECT

In this world of high-quality digital recording, sometimes it's fun to degrade your signal a bit and add that old-school, low-fi sound back to some of your tracks. You can use the technique described below to make any of your sound sources—vocals, guitars, drums, etc.—sound edgy and AM radio-like.

Most of your work in the digital realm will be done at sampling rates of either 44.1 kHz (the sampling rate of a CD), 48 kHz (the typical sampling rate used by many consumer and semi-pro devices), or 96 kHz (DVD-quality sampling rate). Many of these same devices allow you to change your sampling rates, even after you've already recorded a signal or performance.

With your sampling rate set to it's lowest possible option (typically around 10 or 11 kHz), re-record your track or loop—vocals, drums, whatever—onto another track. Doing this will add that grainy texture you're longing to hear.

Another option, especially if you're not yet working in the digital realm, is to run your signal through or into a cheap boom box or cassette recorder, then back into your recorder on another track (use a mic if necessary). Most boom boxes and cassette recorders will not be capable of returning a high-quality signal; therefore, the resultant sound will be a slightly degraded, cheap-sounding compressed signal— exactly what you're looking for.

TRACK 19

In the old days, legendary studios (like those in the Capitol Records building in downtown Hollywood) were revered for their incredible "reverb tanks." These tanks were basically just large, cement basement rooms set up with a speaker and a microphone or two. The engineers of these early studios simply re-amped a signal—that is, they played an already-recorded track back through a speaker—into the reverb tank. Of course, the signal bounced around like crazy down there, creating a wonderful ambience that the microphones were placed to capture. The engineers then took the signal coming through the reverb tank room mics and laid it down on another track, which gave them the reverb sounds that are still renowned today.

You can use this same technique to create your very own reverb tank. Put a guitar amp or some type of monitor speaker in your bathtub or basement, and run a signal into it from your board. Be sure to use a clean setting on the guitar amp (unless you're using this technique to punch up a crunch guitar signal, in which case you can give the dirty setting a try). Place a mic or two in the room to pick up the reverberations, then run that signal back into your recorder. Now mix the dry and reverb signals together to taste. (Obviously, you don't do this with kids, morons, or anyone else around who just might think it's funny to turn the water on and give your amp a bath).

Guitar amp
or monitor speaker

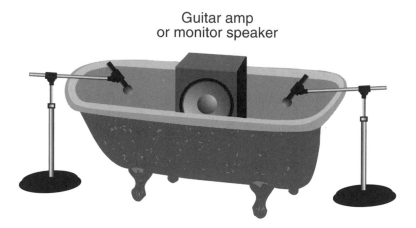

Experiment with different locations in your house for different depths of reverb. Of course, everyone knows that a bathroom or an unfinished, cement basement are best, but you might also find that an empty room or hallway will provide a great reverb sound as well. The stairway between the first and second floors of my house has a great reverb, due to its two-story ceiling. Large walk-in closets, preferably empty, would also create a cool sound. You can even use household items and appliances, such as garbage cans, the inside of your clothes dryer, or a length of rain gutter downspout to run sound through for a touch of reverb. Experiment around your house and you'll find you've got a variety of different-sized reverb tanks and devices at your disposal.

TRACK 20

71 ADD A LITTLE AIR

Loops, samples, and music created primarily via MIDI or entirely without the use of microphones and acoustic instruments are often lacking in any sign of life. You'd be amazed at how much "air" and life you can add to these mixes simply by recording the sound of a completely quiet room—the sense of depth of which will totally surprise you. Once you've mixed the quiet track to your original, bring up the track of "quiet" and you're sure to add an ambience that was previously missing. (Also, consider re-amping your tracks using the technique described in tip #70.

TRACK 21

72 TYPES OF REVERB EXPLAINED

Although there are all kinds of reverb available to us in this digital age, "room" and "plate" are the two types of reverb most often used on audio recordings. Modern reverb units sometimes include "reverse" and "inverse" room and plate reverbs, gated reverbs, and much more. Use them at your own discretion and try different types on different sound sources. Here are some guidelines on their use:

- **Room reverb**. This is the "ambient," natural reverb that we all hear every day arising from any sound source in any room (except an anechoic chamber—a totally dead-sounding room designed not to reverberate), and thus is the preferred reverb for most musical purposes. The "size" and "decay" of the reverb generated is reliant on the size of the room and the reflectivity of its surfaces; for instance, a solid wood floor reverberates more than a carpeted floor, etc. Larger rooms typically have bigger, longer, and more lush-sounding reverb than smaller rooms. Room reverb is great for drums and useful on most musical instruments. Typically, you capture the sound of this reverb using "room" mics, set at a distance from the sound source, and often in a position to capture the sound reflection off a wall.

- **Plate reverb**. This reverb is a manmade creation that is popular on vocal tracks. While these days most of us use digital reverb units that feature plate reverb options on their menus, a *real* plate reverb unit consists of a sheet of metal, a transducer, and a pickup or microphone. An audio signal is run through the transducer, causing the sheet of metal—the "plate"—to vibrate. The vibrations are captured by the pickup or microphone and, *voila*, plate reverberation. As are most metallic items, plate reverb is typically a little heavy on the high-end sizzle; so you might want to roll off the highs above 3 kHz when using it.

- **Gated reverb**. This is great on snare drums and was all the rage in the '80s—due largely to the work of producer Robert John "Mutt" Lange, who used gated reverbs on the snares on his multi-platinum Def Leppard productions. Basically, Lange would use the biggest room reverb he could find then set it for the longest decay available (the amount of time the reverb continues reverberating). Doing so would make the snare sound awesome, but the long decay would interfere with the other instruments. So, right after the snare hit, he'd cut the decay off with a noise gate—hence the name gated reverb. Try it; you'll like it.

TRACK 22

73 REVERB TRICKS

When you first get a new reverb unit, chances are you'll use it on everything—all the time. But resist the temptation to overdo the reverb. Instead, learn to increase and decrease your use of reverb appropriately throughout different parts of a song, and on different instruments; otherwise your recordings will soon have a sameness that you'll come to regret later in life. Here are a few judicial ways to change up your reverb usage:

- **Change reverb settings**. Between verse and chorus, or between verse and bridge, or between instruments and vocals. Don't make everything sound the same, all the time. Resist the temptation to put too noticeable an overall gloss of reverb on your entire recording, or you'll just muck everything up.

- **Take advantage of built-in reverb**. Many studios have several reverb units and dedicate one to each specific track—such as the snare track or lead vocal track. If you have only one unit, you'll probably want to assign it to the lead vocals. But many keyboards, drum machines, and other electronic devices made today have built-in reverb, so learn to use these features to your advantage.

- **Keep it clean**. To keep your recordings cleaner, don't use reverb at all on the accompaniment or cameo instruments. Try taking the reverb off the bass guitar and tambourine.

- **Turn it up slowly**. Listen to your tracks solo as you initially set the reverb on them. Then turn the reverb output to zero, and begin listening to the entire track with all the instruments. Then turn the reverb output up until the reverb sounds good, but not overdone.

- **Panning**. Try panning your reverb returns hard-left and -right for a wide, lush reverb; or straight up in the center for a '50s-style mono-reverb sound.

- **EQ it.** Use EQ on your reverb to customize its sounds. Plug the reverb unit or reverb-laden track through an outboard EQ unit and play around with the settings to create your own trademark reverb sounds.

- **Wet, not dry**. Try a track that is 100 percent "wet"—no dry signal at all. This effect will give a haunting quality to a slow, melancholy guitar or sax solo.

- **Ride the reverb**. At the end of a long, drawn-out note or at the end of the song, turn the reverb up as you bring the level down on the one track or the whole recording. This will give you that fading-away-into-the-distance effect.

74 BAD VIBRATIONS

Monitor speakers will make anything they touch vibrate, degrading the pure sound you'll want for mixing. Isolate your monitor speakers by placing them on blocks, sheets, or wedges of heavy acoustic foam rubber—the black squishy kind. You can track down, purchase, and cut your own pieces to size, or you can buy pre-made products from audio and recording supply outlets for just a few bucks. Either way, keeping your monitors from resting directly on any solid surface in your studio will improve your playback accuracy and add truth to your mixes—helping to eliminate the drastic differences you hear when listening back on other systems. In the absence of foam rubber, you should at least separate your monitor speakers from shelves or whatever they're resting on by placing them on a folded up towel, or even a stack of magazines (like maybe all those unread back issues of *Mix* you've got lying around). Try to deaden the wall behind your monitors as well.

75 EVERYTHING OFF, PLEASE

Turn off your air conditioner or furnace before tracking, especially when using microphones. And don't forget to turn off your cell phone, your land line's ringer, your answering machine, your fax machine, your baby monitor, your remote-controlled door bell, your alarm clock, your timer-controlled lights, your fan, your automatic coffee pot, your pager, and any other noisy contraptions your kids have talked you into purchasing.

Do this before you start tracking—not after it ruins a good performance. If you listen to Jeff Beck's *Jeff* album, you'll hear a telephone ringing in the background on a couple of tracks. Beck told me he was downright disagreeable, to put it mildly, after his engineer let that happen. But Jeff ultimately left the intrusive phone on the recording as an inside-joke-type reminder to that engineer, "for the rest of his life," to never again to let a ringing phone distract an artist during a session.

76 AMPLIFIER GROUND HUM

Ground hum, that low-frequency buzz that often arises from a guitar amplifier, is pretty annoying. If you have this problem and can't get rid of it, try using the low-frequency filter built into most recorders to eliminate those frequencies. Many low-freq filters are set to a fixed frequency; if this is the case with yours, just roll it off. If your filter allows you to set the frequency range, roll off everything in the 100 to 150 Hz range.

77 LAYERING THE MUSICIANS

Late producer Tom Dowd told me that he "arranged" the individual musician's parts as much as he helped to arrange the songs themselves. Dowd would have guitarists—especially those in two-guitar bands or those single guitarists who would overdub multiple rhythm guitar parts—play their parts in different areas on the neck (different voicings, different octaves, etc.) to make better use of the whole audible frequency spectrum.

Dowd would also bring this methodology into play with the keyboard player by asking him or her to separate their right and left hands by as much as a couple of octaves (an unusual playing position much of the time) in order to free up the frequencies in between the keyboardist's hands—a space into which Dowd might then fit a vocal or guitar part. Other times, Dowd would sometimes simply have the keyboardist move his or her left hand down one octave, or the right up one octave, to create the necessary opening.

78 RECORD IT OR REGRET IT

Mark Kendall, guitarist and songwriter of the multi-platinum rock group Great White, told me he carries a handheld tape recorder with him everywhere he goes, particularly in his car, to capture song ideas as they strike him. It's just best to get the idea when it's fresh, rather than hoping to remember it later, like when you get home. The first thing to disappear from his memory, Kendall lamented, was the rhythm—he might have a general recollection of how it was to go, but unless he sang it into a tape recorder at the moment of inspiration, he'd be unable to re-create it later, losing its magic—even when he recalled the melody exactly.

I've experienced this same misfortune myself many times. I might remember how the riff went, or even where it was on the guitar—even sort of what the rhythm groove felt like—but if I don't capture it when the idea first arises, I can't re-create that same feeling, and the riff just won't seem worth pursuing. Since the magic is in the rhythm, without it, a melodic idea is essentially useless. Small tape recorders are cheap. Get one, and carry it with you everywhere.

79 DOWNSIZE YOUR GUITAR RIG

If you're heading into a pro studio to lay down some guitar tracks, or even heading just over to a friend's home studio, you'll probably be more relaxed and perform better if you aren't stressing out over transporting a ton of gear. Downsize your rig as much as possible, starting with your amp. Everyone in the world is using digital amp modelers these days, from top producers and rock stars to your local guitar hero. You should give it a try, too.

Dwight Yoakam's producer and guitarist Pete Anderson showed me around on his Beta copy of Amp Farm—Line 6's software version of their successful amp line—years ago. He's been using digital amp modelers for almost a decade now. In fact, the Blackface Twin in the Line 6 Pod (or whatever they call that patch these days—they have to be careful not to infringe on Fender's trademark) is actually an incredible digital model of Anderson's amp. Not an amp *like* his amp; his *actual* amp. Anderson told me more recently that it's so easy to get a great guitar sound using digital modeling that it doesn't even make sense to plug in an amp and struggle with microphones anymore—and this is from a guy in a musical genre where an authentic tone is golden (or multi-platinum, as it is in his case).

Blues great Sonny Landreth suggests downsizing your guitar arsenal as well. He told me that, instead of carrying around a bunch of differently voiced guitars for the sessions he does with John Hiatt and others, he's simply set up one guitar with an assortment of pickups that help him get numerous tones. So instead of carrying three or more different guitars into a recording session, he needs only to haul one. Using Landreth's suggestion, you might set up a Strat-type, three-pickup guitar with a vintage-styled humbucker in the bridge position, a rail-type pickup in the middle, and a vintage single-coil pickup in the neck position—or whatever your choice of tones and pickups dictates. (Please don't modify a valuable vintage guitar; you'll kick yourself and swear at me later when you discover how you ruined its value. Instead, get a new or slightly used guitar that doesn't really have serious value anyway, then put new high-quality pickups in that.)

When it comes to effects, while the aforementioned amp modelers usually include a solid assortment of effects, it might not hurt to also carry around a multi-effects processor: something that packs a lot of punch in one device. There are plenty of them out there from Line 6 and a bunch of other reputable manufacturers. These things are among the most fun items you'll ever try out in a music store (so get out there and annoy some cocky salesperson with a bunch of dumb questions and obnoxious sounds).

So there you have it: one guitar, one small, digital modeling amp, and one small, multi-effects processor. Pop a couple of cords and a tuner in the pocket of your gig bag and you're all set (no more huffing and puffing to carry a couple of Marshall stacks up a flight or two of stairs while stressing out that the six expensive guitars you left in your van are already being nicked by the scary dude you passed in the alley).

Pete Anderson, guitarist and producer for Dwight Yoakam, has a string of gold and platinum records—even a couple of Grammys—sitting around his recording studio. Pete told me one of his favorite recording tricks, and it's something all of us can readily use (as long as we can get our bass players to go along with it): Pete "foams" his bass guitar before tracking.

He explained that, on the original Fender basses, under the chrome piece that covered the bridge (most basses no longer have these), there was a piece of foam lightly touching the top of the strings, just slightly damping them. Pete mimics this forgotten technology by placing a small piece of foam under the strings of the bass guitar, pressed right up against the bridge. The foam he uses is just high enough to fit between the string and the body of the guitar; perhaps an eighth of an inch higher than the string height (the distance from the body of the bass to the bottom of the string), so that it's gently touching and applying a slight bit of pressure to the strings. It's just a small piece of foam, maybe a quarter of an inch or a half an inch wide. Then, he takes another small piece of foam and tapes it over the nut, barely extending an eighth of an inch onto the fretboard.

Pete insists this will give any bassist "instant technique." The foam removes a lot of extraneous noises on the bass, and will make any bassist sound like a *really* good player. The sound that will result from foaming the bass will be tight and compressed; and from there, if you need to add sustain, you can do so using reverb and delay. But if there's too much sustain in the track from the start (due to the way most inexperienced bassists play) chances are you can't remove it without removing some of the fundamentals of the instrument's tone.

TRACK 23

81 JEFF BECK LOVES LOOPS

Jeff Beck told me that, to come up with the best, most unique riffs he can muster, he jams along with his rhythm tracks—with the recorder on—in five-minute-or-so loops (or about once through an entire song, considering the average length of most of his songs). Then he stops and listens to whether the recorder captured anything he wants to continue exploring or expand upon. If not, he just records again (and again and again), listening after every five minutes or so, piecing together the most creative tracks he can construct. If just one little phrase out of the entire five-minute jam sounds like something he wants us to hear, he'll go back, figure out what he did, and try to build on that.

Like almost everyone else these days, Beck uses Pro Tools to record his albums (though he claims he's looking for a good analog studio in which to get back to basics). And with most of these recording programs (see tip #9), you can easily make notes and place markers by the second, measure, or beat to mark a spot of interest and return there at the touch of a key. So Beck does exactly that; and if he hears something that stands out "a million miles" from what he's done the rest of the time, he'll focus on that, and examine it closely for what he did. Also, he suggests that, to be really original, you need to "look inside yourself, and just start impressing yourself by what you've come up with. Not with what somebody else has done."

82 WAKE UP THE ENGINEER...

It can sometimes be difficult to get past your own humility, or your own ego, to determine when you've actually recorded something of merit. Here's a simple tip from Jeff Beck: He told me that he relies on cues from his engineers and others in the studio while he's laying down guitar tracks to let him know when he's really onto something good. Studio work can be tedious, and people can easily get into a zombie-like state while sitting behind the board or waiting their turn while other band members record their parts. So, if the in-studio audience suddenly becomes more attentive—even by way of just a slight change in their posture or focus—Beck says he knows he's done something that has caught their ear and continues in that direction. You might benefit by doing the same.

83 CREATIVE ATMOSPHERE

Recording studios often tend to be dark, mausoleum-like environments. Most have no windows, minimal lighting, and very little fresh air. No wonder the musicians with the most frightening studio tans are also the best candidates for the loony bin. Don't drive yourself to despair in a less-than inspiring—no, make that a downright depressing—studio; especially if it's your home studio and you can do something about it.

Songwriter Desmond Child has hit the top of the charts more than 40 times within each of the past three decades. He's co-written smashes with Aerosmith, Bon Jovi, Cher, Ricky Martin, Kiss, Alice Cooper, Trisha Yearwood, and many others. Desmond, of course, can afford some of the finer things in life, like a couple of expensive Miami Beach homes he's turned into top-of-the-line recording studios. But during a visit there, I couldn't help but notice how stylish, cool, and *comfortable* the various rooms in his very busy digs really were.

Desmond told me that he highly values a creative atmosphere, particularly when trying to write. He even has rooms decorated differently, to inspire different moods and emotions that may be conducive to different types of material on which he finds himself working. "I like creating atmospheres that help the mind to be creative," he told me. "I think atmosphere has a lot to do with it."

I particularly liked the plush velvet curtains Desmond had hanging on his windows. They were so long they piled up on the floor, like something you'd expect to see on some old Boris Karloff movie set (as soon as I get clearance from my accountant, I'm installing them in my studio). He's also got overstuffed leather chairs and saltwater fish tanks (though I don't really have room for that kind of refinery in my current studio. How about you?).

Wisely, he's stashed his racks of outboard gear away in cabinetry, so no one has to go face-to-face with technology when attempting something organic, like singing. He's got striking oil paintings on the wall, cool pottery and other statuary tucked away in little alcoves, overflowing bookshelves, and massive chandeliers. Again, Desmond can afford this kind of stuff. But if you're trying to make good music—or even a career of music—can you afford not to make your studio and/or creating room as inspiring as possible?

Try your local Salvation Army or thrift store for a bunch of cheap artwork, if that's all you can afford. If you've got an entire basement set aside for your studio, you've got room for colorful couches, life-size statues, and all kinds of wacky stuff. And don't forget how effective a simple paint job can be. Go for it! Let your aesthetic imagination run wild; then watch your musical imagination really run wild!

84 CUSTOM DELAY SOUNDS

Rootsy players like Dwight Yoakam guitarist and producer Pete Anderson are masters at using delay units to add that little bit of slap-back that fattens up their typically clean guitar sounds. Pete gave me this suggestion for customizing the tone of your delayed signal:

"When patching into an outboard delay unit—such as a Yamaha SPX-90, or a Lexicon, or any number of digital delay boxes that you might run into—you're going to have a send and return level, but it's also going to be on a channel. So what you can do then is go on that channel and go up to 8 kHz, and just obliterate everything above it. You can brown it way up, so it's clean and it's quiet, but it's got a much warmer sound to it. You can EQ the delay, and I would do that. I would EQ the returns. A lot of people just leave them flat, and put them in there, and it's just kind of an ugly sound. And the more people do that, the more it's like, generic. So if you get to the board and you delay the EQ returns, then these boxes become a little bit more customized to your taste."

Sounds good to me. Give it a t-t-t-try.

TRACK 24

85 FATTER GUITARS AND VOCALS

Pete Anderson told me he used this technique to fatten up the sound of a steel guitar on one of Dwight Yoakam's records; but this trick will work just as well on any guitar—and probably on any number of other instruments. Definitely try it on vocals as well.

Of course this is a simple drag-and-drop operation using a digital editor, such as Pro Tools or Acid or something similar. If you're still working in the analog world, well, maybe this is incentive for exploring the potential of modern technology.

Pete recorded a steel guitar player onto one track in his Pro Tools recorder. Then he ran that track through a digital amp modeler—in his case, Amp Farm from Line 6. He then duplicated the track onto two other tracks in his recorder, so he now had three identical tracks of steel guitar where he previously had only one. Then he assigned different amp sounds to each of the tracks, such as a Fender Bassman to one track, a Fender Twin to another, etc. That's the beauty or digital amp modeling: you can change the amp patch even after you've recorded the track. Then Pete just selected each individual track in Pro Tools, and dragged them slightly apart from each other on the recorder's time ruler.

"We ended up with three steels of the same part," Pete told me. "And we offset them a little bit by milliseconds, and sort of fattened it, or widened it. Not chorused it, or doubled it. It's just huskier. And the steel player actually called the other day and said, 'Man, I love that steel sound.' And he was flipped."

You'll flip too. Now go get fatter.

TRACK 25

86 THREE COOL GUITAR TRICKS

Sometimes you're just looking for a sound: a special, out-of-the-ordinary sound. Yes, you can find millions of 'em on sample and loop CDs, but here are a few you can mess around with using only a guitar, a pencil, and some foam. Let these examples set your imagination free to explore other possibilities, too. These fun gimmicks were already proved successful by Pete Anderson, who told me he's used them on various albums and other projects.

1. "On the Meat Puppets *Forbidden Places* record, which I produced, there was a song in there where we took—I have an octave-up guitar that was made by Robin, it looks like a little mando-guitar, but it's just a six-string guitar an octave up. So when you play in E, it's the E at the twelfth fret. I had guitarist Curt Kirkwood play that, and we actually slowed the tape down and he played it. And we recorded it direct. That guitar sounds great direct, for that kind of thing. So [when we returned the tape speed to normal] it was way up, like two octaves up from the guitar, kind of like an angel-hair thing. I forget the name of the song, something about 'Sand in her eyes and we're flying,' something like that. It was a real psychedelic song. That came out really cool. That was *very* cool."

2. "I've done wacky things where I've muted the guitar, foamed the bridge—like really foamed it, top and bottom, so it's just like, 'boop.' It almost becomes a kalimba (an African "thumb piano"). It's great for rhythm playing. Although I don't do ska or reggae, it's great for those styles. And surf too. You can throw in a very chunky, percussive sound—it makes the guitar extremely percussive. You can do that direct, and you can throw tremolo or chorus on it, or any kind of wacky thing. But it's a real unique sound with an electric guitar, muted up really good. It's perfect muting though, not like hand muting, which is imperfect. It's a very cool technique, and it's not limited to surf. It can be applied in any number of ways. It's just up to your creativity. I used that on a record called *Stories of the Years* for a guy named John Bunzow, who I produced for Liberty Records in Nashville. I've used that a couple of times. It's a great sound."

3. "I scored a bunch of station ID and show ID's for cable TV network CMT International, and I used an old trick that I'd used on another record called *Salutation Road*, by a guy named Martin Stephenson from England: I made my own hammer dulcimer. What I did was, I took an acoustic guitar, and two pencils, and took the ends of the pencils where the metal bands are around the erasers, and then I would play the strings, like a hammer dulcimer. You could play them with two hands, or you could fret it. Or if you do it on a high-strung guitar, it's really cool too. It's not as fluid and flourishing as a hammer dulcimer, because a real dulcimer has double strings, but if you do that and then add a 30ms delay, and crank the delay up, it's basically a dulcimer. But you're the guitar player, so you're playing it in your guitar world. You can actually play it, play a lick or a line or something that you want to fly around and make a cool little sound with. That's pretty cool. That's fun and it's a new sound."

87 NIGHTCLUB IN A STUDIO

Many a top producer and artist will say they prefer to record live in the studio, not at separate times in a totally impersonal series of overdubs. Tom Dowd was a huge proponent of this technique and told me he primarily recorded the Allman Brothers, Eric Clapton, Lynyrd Skynyrd, Aretha Franklin, and Ray Charles live-in-the-studio with their bands, only overdubbing the occasional vocal or lead guitar tracks afterwards. B.B. King recently told me he much prefers the camaraderie and the outcome of live-in-the-studio recording, too. I think almost everyone who regularly performs live with other musicians feels more comfortable recording as a group, whenever possible.

If you're heading into a larger studio, or if you've got space in your studio to set up a whole band, try this approach, told to me by producer Phil Ramone, who has worked extensively with Billy Joel, Frank Sinatra, Tony Bennett, Chicago, Bob Dylan, and John Coltrane (among hundreds of others). Instead of forcing everyone to deal with the discomfort of headphones (and the subsequent arguments about who should be louder in the headphone mix) have the band set up live, with a live PA system, just as if they're performing in a club. Position the PA speakers as you would side fills; pointing in toward the group (so the band can hear the PA), and not out towards your imaginary audience. Use additional monitor speakers if you must.

Now set up mics as you normally would on the entire band (you'll probably need all the mics you've got for this), and put a couple of room mics on the PA as well. You'll have to watch your overall volumes, and you may need some baffling to create at least some isolation. Also remember that you won't be able to fix any serious mistakes without re-recording the entire song. But you'll capture the band in a situation in which they're probably far more comfortable. Plus, your recording will benefit from the harmonics created by the sum of all the instruments resonating in the room at one time.

88 PRODUCING A COMFORT ZONE

If you're producing other musicians, let them add their own touch to the music—give them a little room to be themselves and don't produce the life out of them, especially if they're experienced players. If you come across as a studio dictator, you're going to make them uncomfortable about their own playing, setting them up for less-than-satisfying takes. Make them feel comfortable and make it clear that you respect their abilities, and your recordings will sparkle with added life and fire.

Slide guitarist Roy Rogers, who produced (and played on) two great albums by blues legend John Lee Hooker, said this about creating a comfort zone in the studio for an artist:

"If people have a comfort zone about what they're doing and they don't feel at risk, and they feel comfortable, then you have the possibility of the music going higher than you ever could have thought possible. And if you just try to organize everything and say, 'Well this is what we're going to do,' it has no possibility of going anywhere other than how you define it. That's no good. Why would you want to do that?

"With John Lee Hooker, I was there to facilitate and just kinda set it up for him, because it's the musicians who play the stuff in a studio. It's not the producer. The producer helps it and facilitates it, hopefully with the set up, but once the people start playing, you can try a little faster or a little slower, or you change something, but it's the musicians. You want to really create a comfort zone. [Of course] I was working with John Lee Hooker, so he was tried and true. If you're working with a young artist, someone who needs direction, that would be a whole different thing. They need more help.

"Also, when you're working with people, you can't be in awe of them. It's about getting the job done. You may think about it later, but when you're there doing it, you have a job to do and you want to do it the best you can. That's the way you get great work."

89 FAKING LIVE AMBIENCE

I've included a couple of tips elsewhere in this book regarding the capturing of the ambience of a complete band cranking away live in a studio. Sometimes, of course, you just can't do that, no matter how great the effect. If you're recording in a small home studio, or if you're the only musician and you've got to play all the instruments, the live-in-the-studio thing is out of the question. Still there are ways to add that live-band feel to your recordings.

Veteran blues producer Dick Shurman has worked with everyone from Johnny Winter to Albert Collins to Robert Cray. Dick told me he likes to work with live bands and complete rhythm sections whenever possible, but when he can't, he imitates the live recording sound by using room mikes on the complete mix.

"Whenever possible, I do like to use room mikes. Usually we've got a couple of room mikes set up out in the empty studio and when we're mixing, we're going to throw the mix out into the room and use the studio to basically serve as an echo chamber. So it's like having room mikes for the actual performance, instead of just the stuff you can originally hear out in the room, which didn't include an amplified vocal or the piano player who is in a booth. Pumping the stuff out in the room after the mix helps you out. It's like having room mikes up without taking the risks of having something in the room mikes that's going to complicate the overdub process later. You get your basic mix happening and then you pipe it out and into the rooms. It's a form of delay."

The cool thing about this tip is that you can use Shurman's technique even in the privacy of your own bedroom studio. Just be sure to turn off your phone, and sit there quietly while you record your playback. Also, with live mics recording the room sound of your monitors, you'll need to be careful about feedback.

90 CABINET BACK MIC TRICK

The art of miking seems to be fading away with the proliferation of digitally modeled sounds available today. The tones coming out of a lot of digital guitar amplifier modelers, for example, include classic miking options already built into the signal. The way things are going, pretty soon no one will actually remember how or where to put an actual microphone—it'll all be done for us digitally. (And then we'll all sound perfect; and perfectly the same. Uggh.)

Here's another great miking tip shared with me by blues producer Dick Shurman. He's used this when miking the many well-known blues guitarists he's worked with. It'll probably work pretty well for you too (even if blues ain't your bag).

Dick told me he likes to put a microphone behind the guitar amp in addition to the close mic and room mic he typically positions out in front of the amp. He does this with both open-backed and closed-backed cabinets.

Here is what Dick had to say about the third mic:

"A few years ago, somebody showed me the surprising virtues of a rear mike. It really adds a lot more bite and bigness than I would have thought. The clarity that I was able to get with a rear mike surprised me. So with a combination of three mikes (close, room, and rear) you've got a lot of ways to get a guitar sound that's a lot closer to the way it's going to sound at a gig."

The only downfall to using a mic in the back of an amp is that you may face increased phase cancellation problems between your front and back mics; so be sure to check for the occurrence of this between the mics, and make any necessary adjustments—beginning with the mic you've positioned behind the amp (assuming you've first dialed in a great sound on your close mic, then on your room mic, before adding a mic behind the amp).

To reduce or eliminate phase cancellation, simply change the position or angle of the mic while listening to the blend of mic signals. And don't get overly stressed over the technology of phase cancellation—when it sounds good, it is good. (For more on phase cancellation, see tip #20). And don't limit this technique to just guitar amplifiers, either. Positioning microphones 360 degrees around any sound source is sure to create interesting sonic options for you.

TRACK 26

91 BIGGER BASS TRACKS

Everybody knows that most bass tracks are recorded direct. But many top producers have told me that they do like to put a mic on the bass player's speaker cabinet and mix that in with the direct sound. Veteran blues producer Dick Shurman explained it to me this way:

"Usually, direct is where you get your definition out of a bass sound, but you get body out of the amplified sound. You definitely need some of both. I don't like bass that sounds too dry and doesn't have meat on it, but at the same time you want it to have shape. You want a tight bottom end. So it's a blend. Usually, the direct signal is in case the sound from the amp is too diffuse and you need to sharpen it up. But the amp is what adds the body to the bass sound."

So there—now your bassist can relax; you aren't going to have to separate him or her completely from his or her earthshaking, wall-of-sound speaker system. And you'll now be able to capture bigger, beefier bass tones as well.

92 SOAKIN' IT LIKE SATCH

Thousands of top recording guitarists, engineers, and producers have embraced digital amp modeling technology. But there will always be those who prefer to use their trusty old amplifiers instead. For many of us, however, cranking our favorite 100-watt head in our home studio is out of the question, especially if we're recording late at night while the family is asleep. For those tone junkies who just can't turn their backs on a Marshall half-stack or Fender Twin in favor of a small bean-shaped collection of transistors, there is another option: speaker simulators, sometimes known as "power soaks."

Joe Satriani told me that, while he plays for hour upon hour, his home studio is kept quiet by a speaker simulator, which takes the place of both his speaker cabinet and the microphones he would normally use to capture the sound of that speaker cabinet. He simply plugs the output of his favorite amp into the simulator, and the output of the simulator into his mic pre and board. The simulator soaks up all the energy the amp had intended for the speakers, and outputs only the tone of the amplifier in a line signal Joe can plug directly into his board. Here's what Joe has to say about it:

"At home, I use a Palmer speaker simulator, which is something that goes in between your amp and your mic preamp. It takes the place of a speaker. That way I can turn my amp to 11, and you can listen to it as loud as you listen to the morning news, which is really great because then you can work for twelve hours and still have ears."

And Joe is not the only guitarist using a speaker simulator to save his ears. Edward Van Halen has long had one in his rack, the Def Leppard musicians use them, and Mike Campbell and Tom Petty use them. Lots of folks have them. Palmer is one manufacturer; there are others.

One of the best things you can do for your recordings is to get yourself a quality mic preamp. Mic "pre"s, as they're often called, allow you to shape and enhance the sound your microphones capture before sending that sound into your recorder; particularly as concerns signal-to-noise ratio. Many mic preamps add compression, limiting, and the warmth of tube technology to the signal. Also, most mic pres supply the phantom power required by many condenser and ribbon microphones. Many stand-alone recorders have built-in mic preamps, but these are not always of the highest quality. Outboard mic preamps can range in cost from as little as one hundred to several thousand dollars; and of course, you get what you pay for.

And, if you're working in the digital realm, but recording acoustic instruments such as guitars, pianos, drums, etc. analog, you're going to need a quality analog-to-digital and digital-to-analog converter (A/D and D/A, or ADC and DAC) somewhere in your signal chain. (And even if you're not recording acoustic instruments, you'll still need to convert your signal from digital to analog for your final mix, at the very least.) Again, stand-alone recorders and most computer sound cards and audio interfaces include these converters; but these built-ins are usually of lesser quality than those that can be purchased separately.

Converters do a pretty obvious job: they convert an analog audio signal into something your computer or digital hard disk recorder can understand—digital data. And on the way back out to your monitor speakers (or for the purpose of burning a CD your cousin Dupree can listen to), that data usually needs to be converted back to an analog signal. High-quality converters do a great job of converting this data back and forth without losing any of the information. However, cheaper converters, to put it in basic terms, don't "hear" so well; they have to guess at a lot of the information they didn't hear correctly, and they make up data to fill in for the signal they didn't quite capture, resulting in a loss of sound quality.

When Joe Satriani set up his home studio, he turned to his longtime sound engineer John Cuniberti for advice on what gear he simply must have in his studio. Joe wanted to be sure that anything he recorded at home was of sufficient quality to be used on his final album releases, which would be engineered by Cuniberti. Not surprisingly, Cuniberti's top recommendations were for a quality mic pre and analog-to-digital and digital-to-analog converters. Here is what Joe told me about his home studio, and engineer Cuniberti's advice:

"I've got a really neat little digital studio. I was very careful and had my engineer John Cuniberti come over months earlier. And I said to him, 'John, if I start to record these things, and I say to you that I want to use this, what would make you feel better, from an audiophile's and engineer's point of view?' And he said, 'Well, what you need is a great mic preamp and a really great D/A and A/D converter. So at his urging, I purchased a Millennia Media STT-1 Origin. It's a really beautiful tube and solid-state mic preamp with parametric EQ and compression. And then also an Apogee PSX-100, which is the A/D and D/A converter, before going into Pro Tools."

The Millennia Media and Apogee products Satch chose represent the offerings of just two manufacturers. There are many mic preamps and audio converters on the market these days, in all price ranges. Get the best you can, and you'll notice a marked improvement in the overall sound quality of your recordings.

94 TIGHTER RHYTHM TRACKS

Virtuoso guitarist Steve Vai is a big advocate of digital technology, and a dedicated Pro Tools user. During a visit to Vai's home studio, he showed me two of his favorite implements for improving drum tracks: Beat Detective and Sound Replacer, both Pro Tools plug-ins. Vai told me he used these plug-ins to fix live drum recordings he had made during the tour on which he recorded his *Alive in an Ultra World* album. If your drum tracks aren't in sync with the beat—or even if the rest of the band isn't in sync with your drummer—these programs (and others like them) may help tighten things up. Here's what Vai had to say about using Beat Detective and Sound Replacer:

"Working in the digital domain, almost anything is possible. I have this program called Beat Detective and it's amazing. It's an extraordinary program for Pro Tools. It analyzes the peaks of all of your kick drums, or snares, or anything that has a peak to it. And you can assign that a beat, so you can actually create a beat. And then if you want, you can shift those beats. You can quantize them or move them around and then they'll cross-fade themselves together.

"I got this program because it was part of a Pro Tools upgrade. Before that, if the kick drum was off from the bass—if they didn't lock—I'd have to go in and cut every little bass note and move it, or cut a snare, or move a guitar. And then when Beat Detective came along, it was like, 'Wow!' It's an unbelievably powerful program that analyzes all the peaks of the kicks and snares, calls that the tempo, and then analyzes the bass guitar, cuts the bass, and moves it to all the peaks of the kicks and snares. You gotta go in and tweak it, but it's just unbelievable what it does.

"And then there is this program called Sound Replacer. So if you have a kick drum that's distorted, Sound Replacer will analyze your kick drum and then replace it with anything you want: nice sounding kicks, or snares, or anything that you have in your sample library."

Ahh, the miracles of the digital age! Of course, similar functions are available in non-Pro Tools formats with other products. Anyone who works with or sells samples and loops should be able to advise you as to which software package is appropriate for your needs.

95 STEVE VAI'S BETTER KICK TRICK

In the modern world, with many of us enjoying having nearly an unlimited number of tracks, doubling tracks and tweaking them differently gives us endless new sonic possibilities. Steve Vai told me he likes to do just that to kick the kick up a notch:

"When I mix, and I have a kick drum, I like to EQ it, so that it sounds like a kick drum. And then I'll take the same kick drum and put it on another track and EQ it differently, and mix them together."

When you think about it, Vai's better kick trick would work with virtually any instrument. Try it on your vocals, keeping one track relatively dry, and adding chorus to the other. Try it on your guitars, EQ'd differently and panned hard-left and hard-right. The possibilities are as big as your imagination.

TRACK 27

96 CONSOLIDATING THE DATA

When you're tweaking tracks in a digital recording system, it's easy to go on and on, endlessly "improving" your recording. Really, at some point, you should probably wrap up the song and move on to the next. Learn to let it go, mate; it's just a song! Of course, before you do that, remember that all those edits and cuts and tweaks you made are eating up your hard disk space.

Steve Vai told me he regularly consolidates his tracks to reduce file size and memory usage and to improve computer performance. Here are Vai's words of advice on consolidation:

"When you're making a lot of edits and a lot of cuts, you're going to have a big mess of little pieces of tracks here and there; so what you can do is consolidate the tracks. It's just a function of the program that allows you to take all of these little pieces that create the channel and consolidate them into one sound file. And that's what I have to do on a lot of stuff because all of the editing becomes memory intensive and the program can't follow all the edits; so you have to sort of consolidate the tracks into something that the computer can read."

In Steve Vai's case, he's using Digidesign's Pro Tools. If you're not using Pro Tools, you may have to search your owner's manual or help menu to determine the best way to consolidate your tracks and the many tweaks you've made to them.

For example, Cakewalk's Sonar suggests that you archive your original file after using the Edit>Bounce To Track(s) command to create a stereo master of the track or tracks in question. Archiving the original allows you to go back and tweak it more, if necessary. But putting that track "away" and continuing on with only the newly "bounced" track, you will save your CPU processing time and allow for better playback and computer performance. Also, remember that unused (muted) audio tracks should also be archived, as they slow down your CPU as well. Most computer-based recording programs allow for this type of consolidation or rendering. Use it to your advantage and you'll save tons of hard disk space.

97 STEVE VAI'S NAKED TRACKS

If you're recording a band live in the studio, chances are you're still planning to overdub the lead vocals and guitar solos (or other lead instruments). While you should consider trying to capture the ambience and energy of the session by laying it all down live on one or two takes (as suggested in some of the other tips in this book), you might also consider recording a few "naked" tracks as well. Naked tracks typically include only the drums and bass, but could include the entire rhythm section without vocals and solos.

With digital editing tools at your fingertips, you can then use pieces of these naked tracks to fix any mistakes on your "whole band" tracks, i.e., in the case that the singer really nailed it but the drummer missed some cues, or the bass player played through a break, or even if the singer or soloist screwed up a bit. Steve Vai told me he did just that when recording his *Alive in an Ultra World* CD. Basically, the majority of that album was recorded live in concert in various cities. But Vai used sound checks to record naked tracks of each tune as well; tracks on which he did not play, but saved in case he needed them.

Here is what Steve told me about how he uses these naked tracks:

"I do this in the event that something sounds really good, but I make a terrible mistake. Then I can go in and take my guitar from a previous night and put it right on top of this track that I'm not playing on, and I do that whenever I can. Fortunately, I didn't have to use a lot of those naked takes, but they're good in the event that I'm doing a solo and I just clam it, or I'm playing a melody or somebody screws up. This way I'll go back to the sound check and pull that part of the song that has just the kick, the drums, and the bass in the room. I'll take a chunk of that song that doesn't have me on it, and I'll cut it into the track, then I'll go back and I'll take a piece of my performance that is good from either a sound check, or another part of the song, or maybe even I'll just overdub it here. And I'll put it right in there and you just can't tell the difference because I'll match reverbs and stuff and make it work. That's called cheating. Don't tell anybody."

98 NONSENSE!

Professional recording engineers and producers have typically laid down thousands, if not tens of thousands, of recorded tracks. Setting up their mixer and recorder and making common adjustments to capture good recordings are entirely second nature to them—simply because they've taken those same mechanical steps so many times.

If you have not done much recording, and especially if you're new to your mixer or recording device—be it computer-based or a stand-alone recording deck—get yourself comfortable with the unit first by simply recording nonsense tracks over and over again, and making various adjustments to EQ, pan, effects sends, punch ins, etc., until the mechanics of laying down tracks on your system becomes second nature to you. This will allow you to concentrate on the performance—essential especially if you're recording yourself. There's nothing more frustrating—or creatively damaging—than having to read an owner's manual and monkey around in endless digital menus between your basic tracks and soon-to-be Grammy-winning vocal tracks. Learn the basic operation of your equipment before you attempt to record your *Sgt. Pepper*, and your recording experiences will be much more satisfying.

TRACK 28

99 DEFRAG AFTER EACH SONG

If you're backing up a stand-alone recorder to an external hard drive, try copying only one song/project at a time to the external hard drive, then defragging that drive after each song. This will compress the data on that drive cleanly, and you'll be able to fit more music/projects on the drive before it's full—and with less risk of lost/damaged file data. And this defragging exercise is equally beneficial—if not more so—if you're recording on a computer.

100 LEARN TO READ, SNEAD

Read more. Recording seems complicated until you read more. Every question you've got has probably already been answered in some book on recording equipment and techniques—including, hopefully, this one.

Visit your local library; they've probably got far more books on recording technique than you would have imagined, and they're free for the reading. (And just so you don't have to strain your brain too much, I'll tell you right now: you'll probably find books on recording in sections 781—near all the books of sheet music, music history, and celebrity biographies—and 621—near books on audio/video, electronics, and home theater—or somewhere close to that).

101 BUY 'EM A BURGER AND A BEER

Beers and burgers serve as excellent enticements to pro and semi-pro engineers with whom you can discuss issues and from whom you can pick up advice. (Of course, you'll have to talk to them at least one time first; you can't just show up at a studio with a McDonald's Happy Meal and expect them to have time for you.) But if you're already hanging out in musical circles, you're sure to run into people who have more recording experience than you— even if they're not pros. And if you're aggressive enough, just go ahead and call some of your local studios and ask to speak to an engineer; then make them an offer they can't refuse. And hey, very few people in the music industry ever turn down free food and drinks—they usually can't afford to.

AUDIO

TECHNOLOGY BOOKS

FROM HAL LEONARD

All About Hard Disk Recorders • *by Robby Berman*

This must-read book for anyone new to hard disk recording covers all the basics of both computer-based hard disk recording systems and studio workstations. Includes thorough, yet engaging and easy-to-follow text, helpful diagrams, and even a glossary of terms.

00331033 ....$19.95

All About Music Technology in Worship

by Steve Young; edited by Corey Fournier

No church musician today is completely prepared to offer their music ministry without a working knowledge of music technology. This book brings you easy-to-understand instructions for everything from synthesizers, MIDI and sequencing to percussion, bass and guitar technology. It covers the history of music technology in worship, hard disk recording, and using music technology in various settings.

00331034 ....$19.95

Audio Made Easy • *by Ira White*

Audio Made Easy is a book about professional audio written in terms that everyone can understand. Chapters include info on mixers, microphones, amplifiers, speakers and how they all work together. Features a new section on wireless mics.

00330260 Book/CD Pack $16.95

The Desktop Studio • *by Emile Menasché*

With the right software, your computer can be a recorder, mixer, editor, video production system, and even a musical instrument. This fully illustrated, comprehensive look at software and hardware will help you get the most out of your music computer and turn it – and you – into a creative powerhouse.

00330783 ....$22.95

Live Sound for Musicians • *by Rudy Trubitt*

Finally, a live sound book written for musicians, not engineers! This book tells you everything you need to know to keep your band's PA system working smoothly, from set-up to sound check right through performance.

00330249 ....$19.95

Loops and Grooves • *by Todd Souvignier*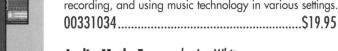

This book surveys the fundamentals and evolution of loop-based composition and explores the power of current groove-making technology. Includes sections on loop-sequencing hardware, loop slicing software, and a CD with examples & demos.

00330969 Book/CD Pack $19.95

Mackie Compact Mixers • *by Rudy Trubitt*

This book provides specific information and hook-up examples on Mackie's most popular models: the "classic" 1202 and 1604; the new 1202-, 1402-, 1604-VLZs, VLZ Pro; and the popular new DFX series. It explains the fundamental concepts of how mixing boards work, emphasizing how audio gets into and out of a mixer so you can begin setting up your mixer to best meet your needs.

00330477 ....$27.95

101 Recording Tips • *by Adam St. James*

This book presents valuable how-to insight that engineers and producers of all styles can benefit from. The text, photos, diagrams, and accompanying CD provide a terrific, easy-to-use resource for a variety of topics, including: equipment • software • ideas from famous musicians • effects • tricks • and much more.

00311035 Book/CD Pack $14.95

The Recording Guitarist • *by Jon Chappell*

This is a practical, hands-on guide to a variety of recording environments, from modest home studios to professional facilities outfitted with top-quality gear and staffed with audio engineers. Topics covered include: guitars and amps for recording; effects; mixer logic and routing strategies; synching music to moving images; and how to look and sound professional.

00330335 ....$19.95

Sonic Alchemy • *by David N. Howard*

This book is an exploration of the influence that colorful, idiosyncratic and visionary music producers have had on recordings. 23 producers talk about landmark sessions including: Phil Spector, Shel Talmy, Brian Eno, Steve Albini and Dr. Dre.

00331051 ....$18.95

Sound Reinforcement Handbook

by Gary Davis and Ralph Jones

This book is the first of its kind to cover all aspects of designing and using systems for public address and musical performance. This revised edition includes: MIDI, synchronization, and an appendix on logarithms.

00500964 ....$34.95

0904